AF608101

THE CATHOLIC UNIVERSITY OF AMERICA
CANON LAW STUDIES
No. 182

The Declaration of Nullity of Marriages Contracted Outside the Church

BY

REV. ADOLPH MARX, J.C.L.
Priest of the Diocese of Corpus Christi

A DISSERTATION

Submitted to the Faculty of the School of Canon Law of the Catholic University of America in Partial Fulfillment of the Requirements for the Degree of Doctor of Canon Law

1943
THE CATHOLIC UNIVERSITY OF AMERICA PRESS
WASHINGTON, D. C.

Nihil Obstat:

LUDOVICUS MOTRY, S.T.D., J.C.D.,
Censor Deputatus.

Imprimatur:

✠ EMMANUEL B. LEDVINA, D.D., LL.D.,
Episcopus Corporis Christi.

Corporis Christi, die XXVIII Julii, 1943.

Printed by
THE PAULIST PRESS
New York, N. Y.

 51

TO

HIS EXCELLENCY

THE MOST REVEREND EMMANUEL B. LEDVINA, D.D., LL.D.

Bishop of Corpus Christi

Assistant at the Pontifical Throne

TABLE OF CONTENTS

CHAPTER IV

CHAPTER V

CHAPTER VI

CHAPTER VII

FOREWORD

HOLY Mother Church, ever mindful of the sanctity of the sacrament of matrimony, has laid down certain norms of procedure which have to be observed faithfully by all those whose office it is to pass judgment on the validity or nullity of a marriage. The procedure itself can be judicial or administrative, depending on the nature of the case. Because of the many difficulties that are encountered by judges of tribunals in applying the laws of procedure to individual cases, the Sacred Congregation of the Sacraments issued a special instruction under date of August 15, 1936. This instruction appeared in the *Acta Apostolicae Sedis*, XXVIII (1936), 312-370. In this dissertation reference is made to this instruction by quoting it either simply as the *Instruction* or as the *1936 Instruction*.

The instruction itself consists of 240 articles. The article discussed in the present work is article 231, which states: § 1: "Si quis certo tenebatur ad canonicam formam celebrationis matrimonii, et tantum civile matrimonium contraxit, vel coram ministro acatholico matrimonium inivit, aut si apostatae a fide catholica in apostasia civiliter vel ritu alieno se iunxerunt, ad hoc ut constet de horum statu libero, neque iudiciales sollemnitates requiruntur, neque interventus defensoris vinculi: sed hi casus solvendi sunt ab Ordinario ipso, vel a parocho, consulto Ordinario, in praevia investigatione ad matrimonii celebrationem, de qua in can. 1017 sqq. § 2. Si quod dubium supersit de recensitis conditionibus in § 1, quaestio ordinarii processus tramite definienda est."

The present work endeavors to give a canonical commentary on each section of the article. The discussion is divided into six parts. The second chapter of the work presents a brief historical outline. An appendix contains sample forms the points of which were gathered from different dioceses throughout the United States.

It is needless to say that the source material on this particular topic is quite meager. Most of the authors are satisfied merely to cite the answer of the Pontifical Commission for the authentic interpretation of the Code, issued on October 16, 1919, and printed in the *Acta Apostolicae Sedis,* XI (1919), 479. This reply constitutes the substance of article 231 of the Instruction.

While the declaration of nullity in case of lack of form is an administrative process, the ordinary, or the pastor who may act in the case after having consulted the ordinary, must always keep in mind that he must do everything that is necessary for obtaining a reliable knowledge about the actual state of affairs as affecting the union under consideration. He must be careful lest he allow parties to attempt a new marriage when in reality a true and valid marriage exists. On the other hand, he must not impede the contracting of a marriage when the parties are free.

The writer wishes to express his sincere gratitude to His Excellency, the Most Reverend Emmanuel B. Ledvina, D.D., LL.D., Bishop of Corpus Christi, to whom this dissertation is dedicated on the occasion of his Golden Sacerdotal Jubilee, for the opportunity of graduate study; to the members of the Faculty of the School of Canon Law of The Catholic University of America for their kind assistance and guidance in the preparation of this work; and to many others for their generous assistance.

CHAPTER I

INTRODUCTION

Lack of Form

By positive legislation certain persons are bound to observe a prescribed form for the contracting of marriage in order to establish externally the internal contractual consent.[1] Lack of form means that these persons disregarded the law by which they were bound, and manifested their internal consent in a manner contrary to the prescriptions of the Church. Lack of form, then, indicates the absence of something that should have existed. Before God the marriage which the parties contracted without observing the prescribed form does not exist. The marriage lacks the appearance or aspect of a true marriage, although the parties may have exchange true marital consent.

In every society certain contracts, because of their importance, require the observance of a specific juridicial form; other contracts, being less important for the common good, may be contracted without the observance of a juridicial form. The juridicial form is so necessary for some contracts that the omission of it renders the act null and void. In other words, as far as the society is concerned, the contract which has been entered into does not exist. The marriage contract, because of its importance, requires the observance of a specified juridicial form, which pertains to the validity of the contract itself.

A marriage defective for the lack of form must be distinguished from concubinage. Concubinage cannot be considered as identical

[1] Can. 1099, § 1: "Ad statutam superius formam servandam tenentur: 1°. Omnes in catholica Ecclesia baptizati et ad eam ex haeresi aut schismate conversi, licet sive hi sive illi ab eadem postea defecerint, quoties inter se matrimonium ineunt; 2°. Idem, de quibus supra, si cum acatholicis sive baptizatis sive non baptizatis etiam post obtentam dispensationem ab impedimento mixtae religionis vel disparitatis cultus matrimonium contrahant; 3°. Orientales, si cum latinis contrahant hac forma adstrictis."

with a marriage invalid because of the lack of form, for it is wanting in the matrimonial consent of the parties. Concubinage may be defined as the habitual sexual relationship with the same person, in the absence of even the semblance of matrimonial consent, which is similar to the use of marital rights enjoyed by husband and wife in the married state.[2] The parties have the intention to enjoy the privileges and rights of husband and wife, but they do not have the intention to exchange marital consent. Therefore, if the parties have lived in concubinage, and one of them wishes to marry a third person, a decree of nullity is not required, because the parties never intended to marry and never actually attempted to contract a marriage.

There are three ways in which parties, who are bound to observe the form of marriage, can attempt to contract a marriage outside the Church. They go before either a civil official or a non-Catholic minister to exchange their consent, or, in States recognizing common law marriages, they simply exchange mutual consent.

However, if the civil law would not permit the observance of the Catholic form of marriage, it is not absolutely necessary that the parties exchange their consent in the normally required juridicial form, for they can at times validly exchange consent simply between each other in the presence of witnesses, as this is granted by the Church under extraordinary circumstances.[3] Since consent is the determining element to bring about a true marriage, it is evident that according to the natural law the parties are capable of contracting a marriage without the presence of an authorized witness. The In-

[2] Noldin-Schmitt, *Summa Theologiae Moralis* (24. ed., 4 vols. in 3, Oeniponte: Typis et Sumptibus F. Rauch, 1936), IV, n. 16; Vermeersch, *Principia-Responsa-Consilia Theologiae Moralis* (3. ed., 4 vols. in 3, Roma: Università Gregoriana, 1933), IV, n. 91.

[3] Can. 1098: "Si haberi vel adiri nequeat sine gravi incommodo parochus vel Ordinarius vel sacerdos delegatus qui matrimonio assistant ad normam canonum 1095, 1096: 1°. In mortis periculo validum et licitum est matrimonium contractum coram solis testibus; et etiam extra mortis periculum, dummodo prudenter praevideatur eam rerum conditionem esse per mensem duraturam; 2°. In utroque casu, si praesto sit alius sacerdos qui adesse possit, vocari et, una cum testibus, matrimonio assistere debet, salva coniugii validitate coram solis testibus."

struction of the S. Congregation of the Sacraments of the year 1936 mentions the ways in which the parties contract a marriage outside the Church, when it states: "... *et tantum civile matrimonium contraxit, vel coram ministro acatholico matrimonium inivit....*"[4]

a. *Civil Marriage*

A civil marriage may be defined as a marital contract entered into between competent parties before a civil official in accordance with the civil law of the country in which the parties reside.[5]

In some countries the parties are bound by the civil law to present themselves before a civil official to exchange their consent before they can be married by a priest or minister of their religion (*Zwangsehe*). As far as the Church is concerned, this civil ceremony cannot be considered as sufficient to constitute a valid marriage, if the parties are subject to the laws of the Church; and the Church strictly prohibits the parties to live together as husband and wife after this civil ceremony and before they have been married rightly by a priest. If the parties thought that the civil ceremony was sufficient to contract a valid marriage, the marriage would nevertheless be certainly null by reason of lack of form, for ignorance would not excuse the parties, inasmuch as their ignorance could never supply the essential factor of the juridical form which did not exist. Inasmuch as the civil law requires the parties to exchange their consent before a civil official, the parties do not violate a law of the Church by thus exchanging their consent, as long as they also manifest their consent before a priest as the authorized witness of the Church.

In some countries the civil law, while requiring that the parties must not only be able and willing to contract a marriage, but must actually contract it in due form, recognizes the validity of a marriage whether the matrimonial consent be exchanged before either a civil official, or a priest or a minister acting as a civil official. (*Facultative Zivilehe*). This is the case in the United States. The parties who come under the ecclesiastical law concerning the form of marriage do not have to present themselves to a civil official. They must

[4] Cf. Art. 231.

[5] De Smet, *Tractatus Theologico-Canonicus de Sponsalibus et Matrimonio* (4. ed., Brugis: Car. Beyaert, 1927), n. 449, p. 390. This work will be cited hereafter as *De Matrimonio*.

be married by a priest in order to contract a true and valid marriage. It is recognized as such by both the Church and the State. They must, however, follow some of the requirements of civil law. In almost all of the States of the Union a license is required before a minister or priest can perform the marriage ceremony. Whether the requirement reflects an essential requisite or merely a legal ordinance depends largely on the fact whether legal recognition be denied or accorded to a common law marriage.[6] In some States the license is necessary for the validity of the marriage as far as the civil law is concerned. The person to issue the license is generally the county clerk. The parties have to appear personally to obtain a license in some States. Such joint examination lessens the possibility of fraud or force. If there is no statutory provision, a third person may be allowed to obtain the license for the parties. The statutes of some States specify that a certain period of time has to elapse between the issuance of the marriage license and the solemnization of the marriage; in other States the parties are required to make application for the marriage a specified period of time before the license is actually issued. Under the latter type of law, they may go through the solemnization immediately upon receipt of the license. In all States a record of the license is kept upon issuance of same in order to have something to show in case the officiant at the marriage fails to return the license after having performed the marriage.

Civil statutes provide which civil or religious officials may perform the marriage ceremonies. Some States require in their statutes that the officiant present his credentials to the proper authority, so that they may be recorded. Before a minister or priest may officiate at a marriage, the parties must present the marriage license to the officiant. In many States the officiant is liable to a penalty if he marries the parties without the proper license. The form of ceremony is not very specific in the statutes of the States. They usually specify that the parties must take each other as husband and wife, and that a number of witnesses must be present.[7]

[6] Alford, *Jus Matrimoniale Comparatum* (New York: P. J. Kenedy & Sons, 1938), p. 200.

[7] Alford, *op. cit.*, pp. 275-277; cf. May, *Marriage Laws and Decisions in the United States* (New York: Russell Sage Foundation, 1929), pp. 14-21.

Since in the United States the priest is recognized as an authorized officiant at marriage, and the parties are not bound to present themselves to a public official, Catholic parties need to observe only the required form of the Church, as they are certainly bound to do, without observing any additional solemnities, except perhaps the addition of witnesses in certain States. Lack of form is present if the parties neglect to observe the required form, even if the parties are bound by civil law to present themselves to public officials.

The question now arises: Can common law marriages be classified under the lack of form cases, in the sense namely, that such unions in view of presenting the appearance of marriages can be declared null because they lacked the requisite juridical form? In order to answer this question a distinction must be made. If the statutes of the State do not make any special provisions, then marriages entered into according to the common law are valid as far as the State is concerned. Before the Council of Trent (1545-1563), the Church required no form for the validity of the marriage; it was sufficient that the parties were willing to contract, were able to contract, and actually did contract a marriage. Marriage then as now was based on the mutual consent of the competent parties. If the parties exchange matrimonial consent in those States which in civil law recognize the validity of a common law marriage, and then live as husband and wife, then one must conclude that the parties contracted a civil marriage, and hence such a marriage may be declared null because of lack of form, for this would be included in the terms of the Instruction of the S. Congregation of the Sacraments. Now, as regards the States which do not admit the validity of a common law marriage, it must be stated that the parties are prevented from just exchanging marital consent and then live together as husband and wife. Therefore, if the parties disregarded the civil requirements of the State in regard to the form of marriage, it cannot be said that they contracted a civil marriage, and hence a declaration of nullity because of defect of form would not be in order. Of course, a thorough investigation into the free state of the parties would be necessary before one of the parties could be allowed to contract a marriage with a third person; but a decree of nullity would not be required, for under the present supposition the parties neither would have contracted a civil marriage nor would they have entered a marriage before a non-Catholic minister.

b. *Marriage Before a non-Catholic Minister*

In the beginning Martin Luther (1483-1546), fought vigorously against clandestine marriages, and he required that a marriage had to take place publicly before it could be considered as valid. However, later he denied that marriage was a sacrament. He claimed that marriage had to be subordinated to the civil authority. From this it follows that Lutheranism must consider every marriage as valid which is recognized by the State as such, even though the marriage did not take place before a non-Catholic minister.[8] As far as those are concerned who are exempt from the form of marriage prescribed by the Church, they are free to contract a marriage according to the laws of the country in which they reside. But the statutes of the different States of the United States recognize the competency of a minister to officiate at marriages. If two parties who are exempt from the law of the Church contract a marriage before a minister, that marriage must be considered as valid, provided that the parties are otherwise capable of contracting a valid marriage, and exchange true matrimonial consent.[9]

However, if two Catholics, or one Catholic and one baptized non-Catholic or infidel, are involved in the case, the marriage entered by them before a non-Catholic minister is null by reason of lack of form, provided that the Catholic was bound by positive law to observe the canonical form;[10] furthermore, Catholics commit a grievous sin because of the *communicatio in sacris,* which prohibits Catholics by divine law from participating directly in the religion of non-Catholics.[11] Therefore, if two parties who are certainly bound

[8] Hervé, *Manuale Theologiae Dogmaticae* (13. ed., 4 vols., Parisiis: Apud Berche et Pagis, 1936), IV, n. 429.

[9] Can. 1099, § 2: "Firmo autem praescripto § 1, n. 1, acatholici sive baptizati sive non baptizati, si inter se contrahant, nullibi tenentur ad catholicam matrimonii formam servandam; . . . "

[10] Cf. can. 1099, § 1, n. 2.

[11] Cf. Triebs, *Praktisches Handbuch des geltenden kanonischen Eherechts in Vergleichung mit dem deutschen staatlichen Eherecht* (Teil I-IV in einem

by the ecclesiastical law concerning the form of marriage present themselves to a non-Catholic minister in order to exchange matrimonial consent before him, the marriage thus contracted is null by reason of lack of form. The marriage, which has been attempted, but which in reality has not been juridically contracted, simply does not exist as a valid union.

Now, it may happen that, in a country in which the parties are bound by civil law to present themselves before a civil official, this office of civil official is held by a non-Catholic minister of the community. The parties must observe the civil law, but they must look upon this civil ceremony as a mere formality required by the civil law, and cannot consider themselves married by means of the civil ceremony as implying simultaneously a religious ceremony at which the minister of religion assisted in his proper ministerial capacity. They do not participate in the divine services of another religion, for the minister is not acting as a representative of his religion, but is merely discharging a civil function which he exercises by reason of his office.

Therefore, whenever parties, of whom at least one is a Catholic and therefore subject to the form of marriage go before a civil official or a non-Catholic minister to exchange their matrimonial consent, the marriage must be considered as null and non-existing because of its lack of the required juridical form, and a decree of nullity must be issued if they want to have this marriage regarded as null.

2. The Nature of the Administrative Process

While the Code does not give a definition of the administrative procedure, it does make a distinction between judicial and voluntary jurisdiction in canon 201.[12] Inasmuch as the administrative procedure is nothing else than the exercise of voluntary jurisdiction,

Band, Gesamtausgabe, Breslau: Ostdeutsche Verlagsanstalt, 1933), p. 245. This work will be cited hereafter as *Handbuch des kanonischen Eherechts.*

[12] Can. 201, § 2: "Iudicialis potestas tam ordinaria quam delegata exerceri nequit in proprium commodum, aut extra territorium, . . . " § 3. "Nisi aliud ex rerum natura aut ex iure constet, potestatem iurisdictionis voluntariam seu non-iudicialem quis exercere potest etiam in proprium commodum, aut extra territorium exsistens, aut in subditum e territorio absentem."

it may be defined as the official act of an ecclesiastical authority in which no judicial formalities or solemnities are observed. This official act is placed upon the request or in favor of an individual. Therefore, the nature of an administrative process is connoted by the exercise of voluntary jurisdiction.

It seems that the canonists of the 17th and 18th centuries had a much clearer idea of the nature of *iurisdictio voluntaria,* and of jurisdiction in general, than is given in the Code. This clear-cut idea of jurisdiction faded during the 19th century, and the Code itself makes a distinction only between judicial and voluntary jurisdiction. It is possible that the authors who wrote on the question shortly before the publication of the Code did not consider this question to be of very great importance for the law. It must be remembered that some of these authors, such as Wernz (1842-1914), and Lombardi (+1908), were pontifical consultors for the compilation of the Code of Canon Law.

Pirhing (1606-1679),[13] divides jurisdiction of the external forum into voluntary and contentious. The former can be exercised only over those who are willing (*volentes*), whereas the latter can be exercised over those who are unwilling (*nolentes*). Voluntary jurisdiction may be exercised validly and licitly outside one's territory. The superior, for example, may dispense his subjects from vows, absolve them from censures or sins, confer benefices on his subjects, administer the sacraments, etc., even outside his own territory, because voluntary jurisdiction can be exercised in someone else's territory without any violation of the rights of the judge of that territory, since the exercise of voluntary jurisdiction does not require a judicial process, even though at times an extrajudicial investigation into a case is necessary.

Reiffenstuel (1641-1703),[14] adheres closely to the opinion of Pirhing. He first explains the meaning of contentious jurisdiction. Then he proceeds to explain voluntary jurisdiction by stating that the latter can be exercised only over those who are willing. Acts of

[13] *Ius Canonicum nova methodo explicatum* (4 vols., Dilingae, 1676), lib. I, tit. XXXI, sectio I.

[14] *Ius Canonicum Universum* (7 vols., Venetiis, 1735), lib. I, tit. XXIX, nn. 8-9.

voluntary jurisdiction embrace also acts of ordination, of consecration and of the conferring of benefices. Voluntary jurisdiction and contentious jurisdiction differ insofar as voluntary jurisdiction can be exercised without the observance of a judicial process, although at times an extrajudicial investigation into a case is required. Therefore, voluntary jurisdiction can be exercised validly and licitly in the territory of another without injury to the rights of the judge of the territory. But in order to avoid the occasioning of scandal or of confusion it is better that it be exercised privately and not publicly. On the contrary, contentious jurisdiction cannot be exercised without a judicial trial; it cannot be exercised in someone else's territory without the express or tacit consent of the judge of that territory as well as the consent of the litigating parties.

Ferraris (+c. 1763)[15] follows Reiffenstuel almost verbatim. He divides jurisdiction into voluntary and contentious. Voluntary jurisdiction can be exercised only over those who are willing; and, as far as ecclesiastical matters are concerned, it comprises consecrations, blessings, the granting of dispensations, the conferring of benefices, etc., as acts within its scope. Voluntary jurisdiction differs from contentious jurisdiction insofar as the former is exercised without any adherence to the rules and formalities of a judicial process, whereas the latter must be exercised in a judicial process.

According to Pichler (1670-1736),[16] voluntary jurisdiction is the exercise of a public power over those who are willing; it is exercised without the observance of a judicial process. Schmalzgrueber (1663-1735),[17] simply repeats the views of the canonists, but he does not consider the question of voluntary jurisdiction in detail. Schmier (1680-1728),[18] defines voluntary jurisdiction as a public power, which is exercised over those who are willing. To the question wheth-

[15] *Prompta Bibliotheca, Canonica, Iuridica, Moralis, Theologica, necnon Ascetica, Polemica, Rubristica, Historica* (9 vols., Romae, 1885-1899), s. v. *"iurisdictio."*

[16] *Candidatus Iurisprudentiae Sacrae* (4 vols., Ingolstadii, 1716), lib. I, tit. XXIX, n. 6.

[17] *Ius Ecclesiasticum Universum* (12 vols., Romae, 1843-1845), lib. I, tit. XXXII, n. 5.

[18] *Iurisprudentia canonico-civilis* (3 vols., Salisburgi, 1716), lib. I, tract. V, cap. VIII, sectio II.

er the assistance of a pastor at a marriage must be considered as an act of voluntary jurisdiction he answers in the affirmative. He explains that previously he had denied the power of jurisdiction to the pastor for the external forum, but that he was only thinking of contentious jurisdiction, and not of voluntary jurisdiction.

Lega (1860-1935),[19] is the only one of the canonists who, in writing shortly before the publication of the Code, follows the authors of the earlier centuries. According to him the power of jurisdiction includes the whole public power of governing. He distinguishes between contentious and voluntary jurisdiction, but claims that acts which do not fall within the scope of contentious jurisdiction need not necessarily be considered as included in voluntary jurisdiction, for voluntary jurisdiction includes only those acts which are not of a legislative or a judicial nature. Thus, Lega differs from the earlier canonists insofar as he excludes the legislative power from the sphere of voluntary jurisdiction. Wernz [20] explains the meaning of voluntary jurisdiction as did the authors before him, but it is to be noted that he does not stress the distinction between the exercise of jurisdiction *in volentes* and *in invitos*. He emphasizes the distinction between the exercise of jurisdiction *in stricta forma iudiciali* and *non-iudiciali*. There is no doubt that his doctrine formed a basis for the distinction between the *iurisdictio iudicialis* and the *iurisdictio voluntaria seu non-iudicialis* which is now found in canon 201 of the Code. Silbernagl (1831-1904),[21] states that ecclesiastical jurisdiction embraces the power of ecclesiastical superiors to govern their subjects. This public power is administrative (*iurisdictio voluntaria*) as well as judicial (*iurisdictio iudicialis*). Many authors [22] limit the

[19] *Praelectiones De Iudiciis Ecclesiasticis* (4 vols., Romae, 1896-1901; Vol. I, 2. ed., Romae, 1905), I, 67.

[20] *Ius Decretalium* (6 vols., Romae, 1898-1905), II, 9.

[21] *Lehrbuch des katholischen Kirchenrechts* (3. ed., Regensburg, 1895), p. 279.

[22] Cf. Gerlach, *Lehrbuch des katholischen Kirchenrechts* (3. ed., Paderborn, 1876), p. 265; Vering, *Lehrbuch des katholischen, orientalischen und protestantischen Kirchenrechts* (3. ed., Freiburg i. B., 1893), p. 673; Heiner, *Katholisches Kirchenrecht* (6. ed., 2 vols., Paderborn, 1913), II, 11; Sägmüller, *Lehrbuch des katholischen Kirchenrechts* (3. ed., 2 vols., Freiburg, 1914), II, 313.

term *jurisdiction* to judicial matters. *Iurisdictio contentiosa seu necessaria* pertains to contentious and criminal judicial matters, whereas *iurisdictio voluntaria* is defined as the authentic attestation (*Beglaubigung*) and confirmation (*Bekräftigung*) of certain juridical acts. Voluntary jurisdiction, *i. e.*, an act to attest to and confirm ecclesiastical matters, is exercised in the Church either through judicial organs or through specially appointed ecclesiastical organs.

The Code of Canon Law speaks of judicial and voluntary jurisdiction in only two places, namely, when it points out the juridical character of these two kinds of jurisdiction in canons 201 and 1507. The treatment in canon 201 offers the greater detail. The true meaning of voluntary jurisdiction must be gathered from this slight indication given in the Code as well as from the doctrine of pre-Code authors. It is imperative, therefore, to investigate also the opinions of authors who wrote after the promulgation of the Code. There are two groups of authors: The first group regards jurisdiction as the sum total of the public power to govern, and it refers to the jurisdictional activity which is exercised in a strictly judicial manner as judicial jurisdiction, and to all other jurisdiction as voluntary jurisdiction. Maroto (1875-1937),[28] is the chief representative of this first group. He states that voluntary jurisdiction is that which is exercised without a strictly judicial form. Voluntary jurisdiction is every jurisdiction which is not regulated by the rules of procedure as explained fully in the first section of Book IV of the Code. Almost all power of the external forum emanates from voluntary jurisdiction. The same must be said for the power of the internal forum with the exception of the sacramental internal forum. Thus, legislative power is derived from voluntary jurisdiction, and legislative power is that power by which laws are made and the social order and life are regulated. Voluntary jurisdiction comprises also that power by which the superior grants dispensations, favors, privileges and indulgences. It is reflected in the exercise of administrative power as well as in the use of governing power. Judicial power, if it be understood formally and theoretically, and if it be exercised not in a strictly judicial manner, but paternally or in an administrative process, as for

[28] *Institutiones Iuris Canonici ad Normam Novi Codicis* (2 vols., Vol. I, 3. ed., Romae: apud Commentarium pro Religiosis, 1921), I, 863.

example, in any of the processes described in the third part of Book IV of the Code, can not be said to be properly judicial, as in contrast to voluntary jurisdiction. It is clear that one may not unduly insist on the word "voluntary" as implying a jurisdiction which is exercised only at the free request of a subject. This definition has indeed been favored by some authors, but it little corresponds to the concept in the Code which identifies all voluntary jurisdiction with non-judicial power. Voluntary power in the law, as the Code states it so aptly, is exactly the same as non-judicial power.

Vidal (1867-1938),[24] fully agrees with Maroto. He repeats the definition given by Wernz, and states that jurisdiction can be divided into judicial and voluntary power. Voluntary jurisdiction is exercised at the request of the faithful concerning those matters which the ecclesiastical superior settles in accordance with his prudent judgment apart from all judicial formalities and remedies of appeal. Voluntary jurisdiction therefore embraces also the legislative and governing powers.

The representatives of the second group consider the meaning of jurisdiction in a narrower sense. They agree with the authors of the first group on the meaning of judicial jurisdiction, but regarding voluntary jurisdiction they disagree insofar as they take voluntary jurisdiction in a narrower sense than the authors of the first group. Eichmann [25] is the chief representative of this group. He opposes vigorously the view held by Maroto, and in defense of his assertion he cites canon 335, § 1, which divides a residential bishop's competence into legislative, judiciary and coactive powers. He claims that by making judicial jurisdiction and voluntary jurisdiction contradistinctive terms, the basis for this distinction must be sought not simply within the realm of jurisdiction as such, but rather within the realm of judiciary power alone. He explains voluntary jurisdiction by pointing out that the one who has such jurisdiction exercises it in favor of or at the request of an individual. The exercise of voluntary jurisdiction (*die freiwillige Rechtspflege*) therefore connotes

[24] Wernz-Vidal, *Ius Canonicum* (7 vols. in 8, Romae: Apud Aedes Universitatis Gregorianae, 1927-1938), II, 364.

[25] *Lehrbuch des Kirchenrechts auf Grund des Codex Iuris Canonici* (2 vols., Paderborn, 1923), I, 121.

simply an act wherein the law lends itself to an application or a disposal in matters which are not contested in court against the petition of the subject for whom the voluntary jurisdiction is exercised. The administrative process falls within the scope of this application and disposal. Voluntary jurisdiction does not include the enacting of legislation, the inflicting of punishments or the utilizing of coactive power. It excludes the settling of all contentious matters for which a judicial process must be invoked. It also excludes ordinations, consecrations and blessings when these acts are considered as implying solely the exercise of the power of orders. To a certain extent, however, the acts of consecrations, blessings and ordinations may be included in the exercise of voluntary jurisdictions, insofar namely as certain juridical effects result from the performance of these acts, such as incardination. Haring [26] follows the opinion of Eichmann.

It seems that the opinion of Maroto must be accepted as being more probable. The reasons are both external and internal.

a. The external reasons:

1. The opinion of Maroto is the same as the opinion of the pre-Code canonists.

2. It is noteworthy that the representatives of the opinion of Maroto, such as Wernz, Lombardi and Vidal, were members of the committees of consultors for the codification of the Code.

b. The internal reasons, which are of greater importance:

1. Inasmuch as the distinction of judicial jurisdiction and voluntary jurisdiction is placed in that section of the Code which deals with the *potestas iurisdictionis seu regiminis,* it must be assumed that it refers to jurisdiction in general. The distinction made by Maroto is quite in line with this general outlook. When Eichmann points to canon 335, § 1, which divides a residential bishop's competence into a *potestas legislativa, iudiciaria* and *coactiva,* he seems not to proceed logically and methodically, and his whole reasoning appears frustrated inasmuch as it does not seem feasible to subordinate voluntary jurisdiction to judiciary jurisdiction to such an extent as to

[26] *Grundzüge des katholischen Kirchenrechts* (2. ed., 2 vols., Graz, 1924), II, 850.

make judiciary jurisdiction the exclusive basis for judicial and voluntary jurisdiction alike. Judiciary power implies that there is something judicial about it. Everything which emanates from that power must be judicial in some way or another. But it is quite evident from the Code that voluntary jurisdiction is strictly opposed to all kinds of judicial jurisdiction.

2. It is evident from the explanations of Wernz [27] and Lombardi [28] why in canon 201 the emphasis should be placed on the expressions *iudicialis* and *non-iudicialis seu voluntaria.* With that assumption there no longer exists any reason for not extending the concept of voluntary jurisdiction in such a way that it will include all jurisdictional acts which are not part and parcel of a judicial process.[29]

In conclusion, since the administrative process is but an exercise of voluntary jurisdiction, therefore the nature of any act placed as a part of an administrative process must share in the nature of an act placed in virtue of the exercise of voluntary jurisdiction.

[27] *Supra,* p. 10.

[28] *Iuris Canonici Privati Institutiones* (2. ed., 3 vols., Romae, 1901), I, 192.

[29] Cf. Hilling, "Die Bedeutung der iurisdictio voluntaria und involuntaria im römischen Recht und im kanonischen Recht des Mittelalters und der Neuzeit,"—*AKKR,* CV (1925), 449-473. Hilling defends the opinion of Maroto. Cf. also Hofmann (*Die freiwillige Gerichtsbarkeit im kanonischen Recht* [Paderborn: Verlag Ferdinand Schöningh, 1929], pp. 64-70), who defends the opinion of Eichmann.

CHAPTER II

HISTORICAL SYNOPSIS

A THREEFOLD development may be noted during the past.

a. Cases which, when they involved a question regarding the validity of an existing marriage, had to be examined and decided in a full judicial trial;

b. Cases which, when they involved a similar question of validity, could be examined and decided by means of a more summary process; and

c. Cases which, when they pointed to the nullity of a marriage because of the non-observance of the requisite juridical form, could be examined and decided apart from any judicial process.

a. The marriage was contracted *in facie Ecclesiae* with the due observance of the juridical form, but there existed a doubt about its validity in view of the possible presence of some diriment impediment in the case. The arguments in proof of the invalidity of the marriage were not evident and obvious. To arrive at a moral certainty regarding the invalidity of the marriage the ordinary judicial process which observed the prescriptions laid down by Benedict XIV [1] had to be followed.

b. In the decision of these cases the invalidity could be demonstrated by certain and authentic documents. The formalities of the Benedictine Constitution could be dispensed with in these cases when they came to the attention of the ecclesiastical tribunal. This dis-

[1] Benedictus XIV, const. "*Dei miseratione,*" 3 nov. 1741—*Codicis Iuris Canonici Fontes cura Emi. Petri Card. Gasparri Editi* (9 vols., Romae [postea Civitate Vaticana]: Typis Polyglottis Vaticanis, 1923-1939. [Vols. VII, VIII, IX ed. cura et studio Emi. Iustiniani Card. Serédi.]), n. 318. Hereafter this work will be cited as *Fontes*.

pensation was in the beginning granted by Apostolic Indult,[2] but later became the general law of the Church.[3] However, the intervention of the defender of the marriage bond was always required when these cases were brought into the diocesan tribunal for trial.

c. The reason for the nullity of the marriage was to be found in the fact that the form of marriage had not been observed by the parties, although the parties were certainly bound by it. The parties contracted either a civil marriage, or entered marriage in a ceremony which took place before a non-Catholic minister, in places and territories where the decree *"Tametsi"* of the Council of Trent had been promulgated. These cases were handled without any judicial process ever since the prescribed form of matrimony pertained to the validity of the act, that is, ever since the time of the Council of Trent in those places where the decree *"Tametsi"* had been promulgated. In the handling of these cases there was an extrajudicial contestation and declaration of facts. In other words, the competent authority had to determine in an administrative manner whether or not the parties were bound to observe the juridical form of matrimony, and if they were bound by it, whether or not they had observed this law when they contracted the marriage. Inasmuch as the process was merely administrative, and not judicial, the intervention of the defender of the marriage bond was never required.

1. Before the Council of Trent

In order to determine the manner of procedure which was followed before the Council of Trent to declare a marriage null when the parties who were bound to observe the form failed to comply with this prescription, a brief historical outline on the form itself must be considered. For, if it can be established that at any period

[2] S. C. C. *Baren.*, 16 mar., 14 maii, 22 iun. 1754—*Fontes,* n. 3644; cf. also *Thesaurus Resolutionum Sacrae Congregationis Concilii* (167 vols., Romae: 1718-1908), XVIII, 25, 33, 41. This work will be cited as *Thesaurus.* Cf. S. C. C., *Santandrien.,* 26 apr., 12 iul., 30 aug. 1788—*Nouvelle Revue Théologique* (Parisiis, 1869—), XX (1888), 627. This magazine will be cited hereafter with the abbreviation *NRT.* Cf. Benedictus XIV, decr. *"Etsi matrimonialis,"* 27 sept. 1755—*Bullarium Benedicti XIV* (3 vols. in 4, Prati, 1845-1847), tom. II, pars II, 287.

[3] S. C. C., instr., 14 dec. 1889—*ASS,* XXXII (1889), 533.

the form of matrimony did not pertain to the validity of the marriage, then it is superfluous to investigate during that period the process for a declaration of nullity on that score. If it can be stated for certain that the form was not required before the Council of Trent to contract marriage validly, then a marriage could not be declared null at that time because the parties failed to observe the form of matrimony.

In a letter of St. Ignatius (+c. 107), Patriarch of Antioch, addressed to St. Polycarp (+166), Bishop of Smyrna, it was stated that the marriage should be entered with the knowledge of the bishop.[4] This is the oldest source which points to a marriage ceremony. However, in this letter no reference is made to a juridical form of marriage as pertaining to the validity.

Tertullian (c. 160—c. 223), informs us that clandestine marriages, that is, such as were celebrated without the knowledge of the Church, were accompanied with the danger of being considered as adultery and fornication.[5]

According to the IV Council of Carthage (398) bride and groom were to present themselves to the priest for the blessing.[6]

The canon attributed to Pope Hormisdas (514-523), insists: "Nullus fidelis, cuiuscumque conditionis sit, occulte nuptias faciat, sed benedictione accepta a sacerdote publice nubat in Domino." [7]

[4] Ignatius Episcopus ad Polycarpum, c. 5: "Decet vero, ut sponsi et sponsae de sententia episcopi coniugium faciant, ut nuptiae secundum Dominum sint, non secundum cupiditatem. Omnia ad honorem Dei fiant."—Funk, *Patres Apostolici* (2. ed., 2 vols., Tübingae, 1901), I, 290.

[5] Tertullianus, *De Pudicitia*: "Ideo penes nos occultae quoque coniunctiones, id est non prius apud ecclesiam professae, iuxta moechiam et fornicationem iudicari periclitantur."—Preuschen's Tertullianus, *De paenitentia, De pudicitia* (2. ed., Tübingen, 1910), p. 24; this is contained in G. Krüger's "Sammlung ausgewählter kirchen—und dogmengeschichtlicher Quellenschriften."

[6] Can. 13; cf. Bruns, *Canones Apostolorum et Conciliorum saec. IV-VII* (1 vol. in 2, 8°, Berolini: G. Reimeri, 1839), I, 141. Cf. also Knecht, *Handbuch des katholischen Eherechts* (Freiburg i. B.: Herder, 1928), p. 605.

[7] Jaffé, *Regesta Pontificium Romanorum ab condita Ecclesia ad annum post Christum MCXCVIII* (2. ed., Correctam et auctam auspiciis Guilelmi Wattenbach curaverunt F. Kaltenbrunner [ad annum 590], P. Ewald [anno 590-882], S. Löwenfeld [anno 882-1198], Lipsiae, 1885-1888), n. 867.

The oldest sacramentaries of Pope Leo I (440-461),[8] of Pope St. Gelasius (492-496),[9] and of Pope Gregory the Great (590-604),[10] contain particular formulae for the bridal blessing given during Holy Mass.

During the time of Pope Nicholas I (858-867), it was the custom for the bridal couple to appear in Church and to receive the priestly blessing. The Pope points out that this blessing could be omitted provided the consent of the bridal couple was manifested externally.[11] Gratian demands for the legality of matrimony: "Horum quaedam sunt legitima, veluti cum uxor a parentibus traditur, a sponso datur, et a sacerdote benedicitur." [12] Alexander III (1159-1181),[13] ordered: ". . . sub anathematis interminatione prohibeas, ne de cetero inter aliquos in absconso, sed publice coram idoneis testibut sponsalia contrahantur." The same Pope stated that a clandestine marriage could be dissolved only if the existence of a diriment impediment could be proved; if such an impediment did not exist, then the parties could be punished because they had contracted a clandestine marriage; but a marriage thus contracted could not be dissolved.[14] Innocent III (1198-1216),[15] did not state that clandestine marriages were invalid. However, he enacted that when a clandestine marriage was entered *in gradu prohibito* (scil., *consanguinitatis*), it should not have the effects of a putative marriage, even though one or both of the parties were ignorant of the impedi-

[8] Feltoe, *Sacramentarium Leonianum* (Cambridge, 1896), p. 192.

[9] Wilson, *The Gelasian Sacramentary* (Oxford, 1894), pp. 265-268.

[10] Lietzmann, *Das Sacramentarium Gregorianum nach dem Aachener Urexemplar* (Münster i. W., 1921), pp. 110-112.

[11] *Monumenta Germaniae Historica* (*Epistolae*, 7 vols., 1902-1925, T. VI, ed. E. Duemmler-E. Perels, 1902-1912), VI, 570.

[12] C. 17, C. XXVIII, q. 1.

[13] C. 4, Comp. I, *de sponsalibus duorum*, IV, 4.

[14] The legislation of Pope Alexander III is not identical with the decree "*Tametsi*" of the Council of Trent. Cf. Freisen, "Die Entwicklung des kirchlichen Eheschliessungsrechts."—*AKKR*, LIII (1885), 103.

[15] C. 3, X, *de clandestina desponsatione*, IV, 3. This is canon 51 of the IV General Council of the Lateran. Cf. Schroeder, *Disciplinary Decrees of the General Council* (St. Louis: B. Herder, 1937), p. 280 for English text; p. 518 for Latin text.

ment. The children born of such a union were to be considered illegitimate.

The Germanic law stipulated that persons had to be married in an open place.[16] The Church followed this during the Middle Ages and demanded that the parties be married *in facie, in conspectu ecclesiae*. The synods of Würzburg (1298),[17] Mainz (1310),[18] Trier (1310),[19] Olmütz (1318),[20] Breslau (1416),[21] and Strassburg (1435),[22] confirm the above statement. Ecclesiastical marriage before the door of the church existed in England until 1549,[23] in France until 1593.[24]

During the 14th and 15th centuries church weddings were almost universal in Italy and in Scandinavia, France, Spain, England and Germany. The nature of the priest's participation in the ceremony was not merely one of blessing but also of solemnizing. But the participation of the priest did not pertain to the validity of the marriage.[25]

From this brief historical survey, since no evidence of a law to the contrary can be adduced, it must be concluded that before the Council of Trent a marriage was contracted validly, even though the parties did not observe any of the ceremonies required for merely

[16] Friedberg, *Das Recht der Eheschliessung in seiner geschichtlichen Entwicklung* (Leipzig, 1865), pp. 17-30.

[17] Hartzheim, *Concilia Germaniae quae celsissimi principis Ioannis Mauritii . . . sumptu Ch. J. Fr. Schannat magna ex parte primum collegit* (11 vols. in Folio, Coloniae Augustae Agrippinensium: J. W. Krakamp, 1759-1790), IV, 30.

[18] *Ibid.*, 149.

[19] *Ibid.*, 207.

[20] *Ibid.*, 272.

[21] *Ibid.*, V, 155.

[22] *Ibid.*, 238.

[23] Bridges (*History of Northamptonshire* [Oxford, 1791], I, 135) speaks of a marriage which took place in the year 1278 as follows: "Robert Fitz Royer in the 6th Ed. 1. entered into an engagement with Robert de Tybetot to marry, within a limited time, John, his son and heir, to Hewisia, the daughter of the said Robert de Tybetot, to endow her at the church-door, on her wedding-day, with lands amounting to the value of one hundred pounds per annum."

[24] Friedberg, *op. cit.*, p. 60.

[25] Triebs, *Handbuch des kanonischen Eherechts*, p. 561.

lawful marriage by bishops, councils or synods. The parties contracted a valid marriage through the exchange of their mutual consent. The different decrees ordained that this consent be manifested externally in some kind of ceremony. However, the ceremony itself did not pertain to the validity of the marriage. Some sort of external manifestation was necessitated by the fact that many parties contracted a clandestine marriage, and afterwards separated only to attempt to contract another marriage. The Church had to take certain measures to suppress this abuse which was occasioned by clandestine marriages, but these measures did not affect the validity of the clandestine marriage provided that the parties exchanged a true matrimonial consent and that no impediment existed to prevent the parties from contracting a valid marriage.[26]

The Council of Trent prescribed a certain and determined form for the valid contraction of marriage.[27] The marriage was null, that is, non-existing, if the prescriptions of the Tridentine decree were disregarded. While the decree condemned anyone who denied that true marriage is brought about by the consent of the parties, it stated that the validity or nullity of the marriage depended by positive ecclesiastical law on the observance or non-observance of the juridical form. The Council deplored the fact that so many, having left the first wife with whom they had contracted marriage secretly, publicly married another and lived with her in continual adultery. Since the Church, which does not judge what is hidden, could not correct this evil unless a more efficacious remedy was applied, therefore, following in the footsteps of the Lateran Council celebrated under Innocent III,[28] it commanded, that in the future, before a marriage was to be contracted, the proper pastor of the contracting parties should publicly announce three times in church, during the celebration of the Mass on three successive festival days, the names of those between whom marriage was to be contracted. After these publications, if no legitimate impediment was revealed, the marriage

[26] Friedberg, *Das Recht der Eheschliessung*, pp. 203-205; Portmann, *Wesen und Unauflöslichkeit der Ehe* (Emsdetten, Westfalen: Heinrich und J. Lechte, 1938), p. 92 ff.

[27] Conc. Trident., sess. XXIV, *de ref. matrim.*, c. 1.

[28] C. 3, X, *de clandestina desponsatione*, IV, 3. Can. 51 of the Council.

ceremony could take place in the presence of the people, where the parish priest was to hear the mutual consent of the parties.[29]

The decree declared that in certain circumstances a dispensation from the publication of the banns could be granted. The decree explicitly stated: "Those who shall attempt to contract marriages otherwise than in the presence of the parish priest or of another priest authorized by the parish priest or by the ordinary and in the presence of two or three witnesses, the holy Council renders absolutely incapable of thus contracting marriage and declares such contracts null. . . ." [30]

Before the decree could have its full binding force, it had to be published in every separate parish. This peculiar form of promulgation was intended to avoid rendering the marriages of heretics null by reason of lack of form.[31] In many places the decree was never promulgated. In such places the parties were not bound by the juridical form of matrimony as laid down in the decree, and if the parties contracted a clandestine marriage it was certainly valid, provided that they exchanged true matrimonial consent and no impediment was present.[32]

2. After the Council of Trent

In the year 1852 the official of the ecclesiastical tribunal of the diocese of Trier, Germany, submitted to the Holy See a doubt about a marriage which was null by reason of clandestinity.[33] The question

[29] Conc. Trident., sess. XXIV, *de ref. matrim.*, c. 1. Cf. Schroeder, *Canons and Decrees of the Council of Trent* (St. Louis: B. Herder, 1941), pp. 183-185, for an English translation of the decree *"Tametsi."*

[30] "Qui aliter, quam praesente parocho vel alio sacerdote, de ipsius parochi vel sui ordinarii licentia, et duobus vel tribus testibus matrimonium contrahere attentabunt, eos sancta synodus ad sic contrahendum omnino inhabiles reddit, et huiusmodi contractus irritos et nullos esse decernit, prout eos praesenti decreto irritos facit et annullat."—Conc. Trident., sess. XXIV, *de ref. matrim.*, c. 1; cf. Schroeder, *op. cit.*, p. 184.

[31] Triebs, *op. cit.*, p. 562.

[32] Cf. Schroeder, *op. cit.*, p. 185.

[33] S. C. C., *Treviren.*, 18 dec. 1852, 29 ian. 1853—"Utrum nimirum sa. me. Benedict. XIV. const. *'Dei miseratione'* . . . etiam quoad illas nuptias sit servanda, quae per se pro ecclesiasticis matrimoniis nullo pacto haberi queunt,

dealt with marriages which *per se* cannot be considered as ecclesiastical marriages, because they were not contracted *in facie ecclesiae.* The official pointed out the laboriousness connected with establishing the nullity of clandestine marriages if the Constitution of Benedict XIV had to be observed in detail. He correspondingly asked the S. Congregation of the Council whether the Benedictine Constitution *"Dei miseratione"* had to be observed when a decision was to be rendered in a case of evident nullity because of lack of form. The official, it is to be observed, did not contemplate the case in which one had a reasonable doubt about the promulgation of the decree *"Tametsi"* in a particular place, or in which one doubted about a certain person's obligation to observe the Tridentine decree in view of the contraction of a marriage with a person who was not bound by it. The S. Congregation declared that there was no obligation to observe the Constitution of Benedict XIV in the case submitted.[34]

The answer of the S. Congregation of the Council was of vast importance, for it distinguished, at least implicitly, between an existing but invalid marriage (*matrimonium irritum*) and a non-existing or null marriage (*matrimonium nullum*). From this response one had to conclude that the Benedictine Constitution was the common law as applied to the hearing and deciding of matrimonial cases and that it always remained in force. One had to conclude also that it was not necessary to follow the Benedictine Constitution in any decision concerning such cases of marriages which were undoubtedly null by reason of lack of form, and which were contracted either civilly or before a non-Catholic minister between Catholics certainly subject to the Tridentine form.[35]

However, the Benedictine Constitution had to be observed if the nullity or non-existence of the marriage by reason of lack of form was doubtful. This doubt arose, for example, when there was

ex eo quod neque in facie Ecclesiae, neque in alia in foro Ecclesiae quomodocumque valida forma contractae fuere."—*Thesaurus,* CXII (1853), 17-23. Cf. also Lingen-Reuss, *Causae selectae in S. C. Card. Concilii Trid. interpretum propositae per summaria precum ab anno 1823 usque ad annum 1869* (Ratisbonae, 1871), pp. 890-897.

[34] "In casu prout proponitur, negative."—*Thesaurus,* CXII (1853), 18.

[35] Feije, *De Impedimentis et Dispensationibus Matrimonialibus* (3. ed., Lovanii: Typis Caroli Peeters, 1885), pp. 485-491.

a question of a marriage contracted by two Protestants, or by parties of whom one was a Protestant and the other a Catholic. Such a doubt could also arise when the parties married civilly and it thereupon had to be decided whether the decree *"Tametsi"* was in full force in the particular locality where the civil marriage was entered into.[86]

The official of the diocese of Trier pointed out that the employment of the ordinary process in such cases of evident nullity would constitute a danger to the parties through the delay which would be occasioned thereby. Furthermore, it would be a burden for the parties if they could contract a new marriage only after two consecutive and conformable sentences had been rendered.[87]

The S. Congregation of the Council considered the possibility that in such cases as the one submitted by the official there could exist a doubt, and it was at first rather reluctant to give the answer: "In casu prout proponitur, negative." The S. Congregation argued as follows: Because of the difficulties arising from the peculiar form of promulgation for the decree *"Tametsi,"* marriages which were null by reason of lack of form were subjected to a doubt about the validity of the marriage contract, which contract could not be separated from the marriage in its character of a sacrament. For these reasons the S. Congregation thought it better to apply the prescriptions of the Benedictine Constitution to these cases, lest the importance of the sacrament of matrimony be thoughtlessly endangered and thus serious harm caused to the salvation of souls. To safeguard the sacrament was more important than to consider the wishes and conveniences of the parties.

However, this reasoning of the S. Congregation could pertain only to a case of doubt. Benedict XIV had ordered in his Constitution that the defender of the marriage bond be present ". . . quotiescumque contigerit, matrimoniales causas super validitate vel nullitate coram legitimo iudice disceptari."[88]

In this sentence the terms *validitas* and *nullitas* stand in contraposition. From this fact alone one could have concluded, perhaps,

[86] Feije, *op. cit.*, p. 491.

[87] Lingen-Reuss, *Causae selectae*, p. 890.

[88] Benedictus XIV, const. *"Dei miseratione,"* 3 nov. 1741, 6—*Fontes*, n. 318.

that *nullitas* was to be understood in the sense of *invaliditas,* especially since the Constitution does not use the term *invaliditas.* If this conclusion had been correct, then the prescriptions of Benedict XIV would have applied to processes of all cases of invalid marriages. However, to attach to the term *nullitas* such a general meaning could not have been the intention of the Pope, since it would have defeated the very purpose of the decree itself. If the terms *nullitas* and *validitas* were employed as contradictory notions, it did not necessarily follow that the word *nullitas* was equivalent in sense to the word *invaliditas. Nullitas* connotes the non-existence of a thing (nullum—non-existens) hence it predicated neither the fact of validity nor the fact of invalidity. The thing which is designated as null simply does not exist. On the other hand, the term *invaliditas* gives expression to the nature of a thing that is in existence. Thus a marriage can be actually invalid because of the presence of some diriment impediment for which no effective dispensation was obtained, even though the parties of that marriage would have complied fully with whatever juridical form was requisite for establishing the validity of the matrimonial contract.[89] From this it is evident that the term *validitas* was correctly employed by Benedict XIV to refer to the juridical status of a marriage which lacked validity, whereas the term *nullitas* was properly used to refer to a union which was devoid of all juridical status. If there was a doubt about the nullity of a marriage, it was the office of the judge to remove the doubt so that its nullity or validity could become certified not only in fact but also in law. In such cases the prescriptions of the Benedictine Constitution had to be observed. This was the conclusion reached by the S. Congregation of the Council in the case submitted by the official of the ecclesiastical tribunal of the diocese of Trier. But inasmuch as the official did not mention anything about a doubt in the case proposed, the S. Congregation felt justified to answer: "In casu prout proponitur, negative."

In the year 1888 the Holy Office ordered the following indult to be sent to the bishop of Angoulême:

> Dummodo agitur de impedimentis consanguinitatis, affinitatis ex copula licita, cognationis spiritualis, ligaminis, disparitatis

[89] Heck, *Der Eheverteidiger im kanonischen Eheprozess* (Bonn: Ludwig Röhrscheid Verlag, 1937), p. 48.

cultus, (dummodo non agatur de valore baptismi forsitan collati, quo in casu recurrendum semper erit ad Sanctam Sedem), et clandestinitatis; atque ex authenticis documentis vel ex testibus fide dignis certo omnino constet de existentia impedimenti, et de dispensatione aut sanatione super eo non concessa, supplicandum Sanctissimo pro facultate procedendi ad sententiam definitivam absque appelatione, non servata formae Benedictinae constitutionis "Dei miseratione," adhibito tamen et audito in singulis casibus matrimonialis vinculi defensore.[40]

This indult made possible the institution of a new summary procedure, for the ordinary could declare a formless marriage invalid, if he could acquire moral certainty regarding its lack of form either through documentary evidence or through trustworthy witnesses. The Benedictine Constitution did not have to be observed, but the defender of the marriage bond had to intervene.

The concession made to the bishop of Angoulême in the year 1888 was in the nature of a particular indult. However, in the year 1889 the Holy Office extended the import of this indult to the universal Church by way of a general decree.[41]

The decree stated:

Quando agitur de impedimento disparitatis cultus, et evidenter constat unam partem esse baptizatam, et alteram non fuisse baptizatam; quando agitur de impedimento ligaminis, et certo constat primum coniugem esse legitimum et adhuc vivere; quando denique agitur de consanguinitate aut affinitate ex copula licita, aut etiam de cognatione spirituali, vel de impedimento clandestinitatis in locis ubi decretum Trident. *Tametsi* publicatum est, vel uti tale diu observatur, dummodo ex certo et authentico documento, vel in huius defectu, ex certis argumentis evidenter constet de existentia huiusmodi impedimentorum super quibus Ecclesiae auctoritate dispensatum non fuerit; hisce in casibus praetermissis solemnitatibus in Constitutione Apostolica *Dei miseratione* requisitis, matrimonium poterit ab Ordinariis declarari nullum, cum interventu tamen defensoris vinculi matrimonialis, quin opus sit secunda sententia.[42]

[40] S. C. C. Off. (*Engolismensi*), 5 sept. 1888—*NRT*, XXVI (1894), 261.

[41] S. C. C. Off., decr., 5 iun. 1889—*Fontes*, n. 1118. Cf. S. C. S. Off., 14 febr. 1894—"An decretum S. Officii, 5 iunii 1889, quo in nonullis causis matrimonialibus derogatur solemnitatibus Constitutionis Benedictinae, sit generale nec ne? R. Affirmative."—*Fontes*, n. 1168.

[42] S. C. S. Off., decr., 5 iun. 1889—*Fontes*, n. 1118.

This decree, just as the concession granted to the bishop of Angoulême, did not distinguish expressly between marriages which are null and marriages which are invalid (*nullum—irritum*). But it spoke of the impediment of clandestinity together with the other diriment impediments, and hence it seems that no distinction was made. But in view of the practice which existed before the publication of the decree, namely, to require no judicial process in questions of evident nullity by reason of lack of form in a territory in which the decree "*Tametsi*" had been promulgated, it is quite evident that a distinction did exist, and the concession to the bishop of Angoulême and the decree of 1889 have to be interpreted accordingly. The Church held to this practice, as is evident from the doubt proposed by the Archbishop of Cologne, in the year 1891.[43] But the question indicates that the Archbishop of Cologne either had not heard of the declaration of 1889, or doubted about its application to mixed marriages.

The second part of the doubt which he proposed inquired whether a summary process could be used in the investigation of civil marriages of Catholics with non-Catholics. In its response of July 2, 1892, the Holy Office did not refer to the general declaration of 1889, but granted a quinquennial faculty for proceeding extrajudicially, with the intervention of the defender of the bond. The defender of the bond in the ecclesiastical tribunal was to act according to the rules of his office, and so it seems that a second sentence was required, since the case had to be appealed by the defender of the marriage bond who intervened in each case of this kind, inasmuch as there were special difficulties involved in those civil marriages which were contracted by parties of mixed religion. These same difficulties probably suffice to explain why only a five-year faculty was granted, despite the existence of a particular response which granted even greater concessions.[44]

[43] Cf. *NRT,* XXVI (1894), 23-36. The decree "*Tametsi*" had been promulgated in the province of Cologne and hence was in force.

[44] "II. Qua summaria ratione idem processus instrui valeat praeter normas in Benedictina Const. praestitutas?" "Ad II. Supplicandum SSmo. pro gratia ad quinquennium dummodo numquam deficiat matrimonii defensor, qui munere fungatur ad tramites iuris, et extraiudicialibus saltem actis atque omni alio quo fieri poterit modo suppleatur, ut ita numquam desint clarae concludentesque probationes."—*NRT,* XXVI (1894), 23-24.

From this it can easily be seen that the Holy Office did imply a distinction in cases and prescribed a different procedure for the different cases. If a marriage was null because the Catholic parties neglected to observe the juridical form in a place that was certainly bound by the law on the form of marriage, then the S. Congregation of the Council granted in a particular case the faculty to proceed without a judicial process, that is, administratively. But in cases of doubt, either about the personal obligation of the parties, or about the promulgation of the decree *"Tametsi"* in a particular territory, the sentence had to be given in the manner indicated by the instructions which the Holy Office had issued. If the decree of 1889 as well as the concession granted to the bishop of Angoulême are understood in this manner, they do not contradict the practice of the Church in regard to the lack of form procedure.

The following distinction can accordingly be maintained. In a question about a marriage yet to be contracted a diligent investigation had to be made extrajudicially for determining the free status of the parties. This was precisely the point which needed determination in the defect of form cases. But when there was question of a marriage already contracted and it was to be declared invalid by reason of the presence of some diriment impediment, then the Holy Office declared that the solemnities of the Benedictine Constitution did not have to be followed, in view of the decree of 1889.[45] In making this distinction it was admitted that an investigation of the free status of the parties prior to the contracting of a marriage was of its very nature administrative, and that, therefore, the entire process was of a purely administrative character.

A last pre-Code response concerning marriages which were null because of lack of form, given on March 27, 1901, was sent to several French bishops. These doubts contemplated the following cases: a marriage vitiated in its contractual form because of the assistance thereat by a priest who was not the proper pastor of the contracting parties; a marriage for the celebration of which the parties attempted *in fraudem legis* to escape from the requirement of the law on the form of marriage by going to a territory where the law was not in effect; a marriage celebrated by the parties in the presence of a non-

[45] Cf. S. C. S. Off. (Albanen. in America), 10 iun. 1896—*Fontes,* n. 1180.

Catholic minister or a civil magistrate. Regarding these cases the bishops asked whether the summary process which did not entail the need of an appeal when judgment was rendered could lawfully be employed. The Holy Office merely reasserted the decree of 1889, noting that it could be used as often as the impediment of clandestinity was clearly proved. The decision whether such proof actually obtained in the individual case was left to the judgment of the ordinaries.[46]

This answer must receive the same interpretation as the decree of 1889. If the marriage was evidently null by reason of lack of form, then the administrative procedure could be employed; but if the nullity of the marriage could be doubted, then the formalities of the Benedictine Constitution had to be followed, and the defender of the marriage bond had to appeal the case.

The practice of deciding all evidently null marriages in an administrative manner remains the same after the promulgation of the Code of Canon Law. This is evident from an answer given shortly after the promulgation of the Code,[47] which answer reflects the whole

[46] S. C. S. Off., 27 mart. 1901—"R. Provisum per decretum S. R. et U. Inquisitionis 5 Iunii 1889, quod intelligendum est tantum de causis, in quibus certo et evidenter constet de impedimentis, de quibus agitur; quae certitudo se desit, a defensore vinculi matrimonialis ad secundum instantiam procedendum erit."—*Fontes,* n. 1251.

[47] Pontificia Commissio ad Codicis Canones authentice Interpretandas, 16 oct. 1919, n. 17—"Utrum Ordinarius, praetermissis iuris sollemnitatibus in Constitutione apostolica *Dei miseratione* requisitis, matrimonium possit declarare nullum cum interventu tamen defensoris vinculi matrimonialis, quin opus sit secunda sententia, hisce in casibus, nempe: 1. si duo catholici, in loco certe antehac obnoxio capiti *Tametsi* Concilii Tridentini, vel post decretum *Ne temere,* matrimonium civile tantum inierunt, omisso ritu ecclesiastico, et, obtento civili divortio, novum in Ecclesia inire student matrimonium, vel novum matrimonium, civiliter initum, in foro Ecclesiae convalidare; 2. aut catholica pars, quae cum acatholica, spretis Ecclesiae legibus, in templo sectae protestanticae (in loco certe antehac obnoxio capiti *Tametsi* Concilii Tridentini, et ubi Benedictina declaratio extensa non est, vel post decretum *Ne temere*) matrimonium contraxit, obtento civili divortio, in facie Ecclesiae novum matrimonium cum catholico consorte inire vult; 3. aut apostatae a fide catholica, qui in apostasia civiliter vel ritu alieno se iunxerunt, obtento civili divortio, poenitentes ad Ecclesiam redire et cum parte catholica alteras nuptias in Ecclesia celebrare desiderant." "R.—Casus supra memorati nullum iudicialem processum requirunt

teaching of the Church on this question. This answer was embodied as Article 231 in the Instruction emanating from the offices of the S. Congregation of the Sacraments in the year 1936.[48]

aut interventum defensoris vinculi, sed resolvendi sunt ab Ordinario ipso, vel a parocho, consulto Ordinario, in praevia investigatione ad matrimonii celebrationem, de qua in canone 1019 et seqq."—*AAS,* XI (1919), 479. Hereafter abbreviated Pont. Comm. Intr.

[48] S. C. de Sacramentis, instr., 15 aug. 1936—*AAS,* XXVIII (1936), 312-361; in particular, p. 359. Cf. Doheny, *Practical Manual for Marriage Cases* (Milwaukee: The Bruce Publishing Company, 1938), p. 115.

CHAPTER III

THE PARTIES IN THE CASE

THIS chapter will consider the parties who are permitted to introduce the case whereby the competent authority is petitioned for a decree of nullity of the marriage contracted outside the Church. Since the procedure is purely administrative, the rules and regulations concerning the parties in a judicial process cannot be applied. The party who signs the petition for a decree of nullity cannot be called the plaintiff, neither can the second party in the case be called the defendant, because these terms are proper to a judicial process.[1] But the proper term designating the one who petitions the competent authority for a declaration of nullity is *orator* (*oratrix*), petitioner; and the other party in the case is called the *pars conventa*, respondent. If both parties concur in petitioning the competent authority for a declaration of nullity, they are called the *oratores* or petitioners.

1. MEMBERS OF THE LATIN RITE.

It is a general rule in law that those who are baptized in accordance with the ceremonies of the Latin rite belong also the Latin rite in the Church.[2] An exception to this general rule is noted for only the following three cases:

a. If the baptism was administered fraudulently by a minister of another rite. The expression *fraudulently* means that the baptism was administered unjustly by a minister of another rite. This includes not only the case in which a child was baptized by a minister of another rite in order to make the child a member of that rite, but also the case in which the child was baptized in another rite at

[1] Cans. 1646 ss.

[2] Can. 98, § 1: "Inter varios catholicos ritus ad illum quis pertinet, cuius caeremoniis baptizatus fuit, nisi forte baptismus a ritus alieni ministro vel fraude collatus fuit, vel ob gravem necessitatem, cum sacerdos proprii ritus praesto esse non potuit, vel ex dispensatione apostolica, cum facultas data fuit ut quis certo quodam ritu baptizaretur, quin tamen eidem adscriptus maneret."

the unlawful request of the parents. This is evident from a response of the Pontifical Commission for the Authentic Interpretation of the Code.[3] This Commission was asked: "Whether those who, at the request of their parents, contrary to the prescription of canon 756, have been baptized by a minister of a rite not their own, belong to the rite in which they were actually baptized, or to the rite in which according to the prescription of canon 756 they should have been baptized. In reply the Commission stated: As the question is put, in the negative to the first part; in the affirmative to the second."[4] This means that the children thus baptized belong to the rite in which they should have been baptized according to canon 756. In such a case it is immaterial whether the parents acted in good or bad faith.[5]

b. If the baptism was administered by a minister of another rite in a case of necessity, because the child could not easily be taken to a minister of its own rite. A case of necessity is present if there is danger of death, or if the administration of the sacrament will be delayed for an uncertain but considerable length of time.

c. If by reason of an Apostolic Indult someone were baptized in a certain rite without becoming a member of that rite.

Children must be baptized in accordance with the ceremonies of that rite to which the parents of the children belong.[6] Inasmuch as the canon speaks of children, anyone who has reached the use of reason, and is therefore to be considered as an adult with reference to the matter of baptism, may ask to be baptized in the rite of his own choice, and thus gain membership in that rite.[7] If one of the

[3] Pont. Comm. Intr., 16 oct. 1919, n. 11: "D.—Utrum qui ad preces parentum, contra praescriptum canonis 756, a ritus alieni ministro baptizati sunt, pertineant ad ritum in quo sunt baptizati, vel ad ritum in quo, iuxta praescriptum canonis 756, baptizari debuissent. R.—Prout casus exponitur, negative ad primam partem, affirmative ad secundam."—*AAS,* XI (1919), 478.

[4] Bouscaren, *The Canon Law Digest* (2 vols. and 1938 and 1941 supplements, Milwaukee: The Bruce Publishing Company, 1934), I, 85, under can. 98.

[5] Cappello, *Summa Iuris Canonici* (3 vols., Vols. I and II, 3. ed., 1938-1939; Vol. III, 1936, Romae: Apud Aedes Universitatis Gregorianae, 1936-1939), I, n. 205.

[6] Can. 756, § 1: "Proles ritu parentum baptizari debet."

[7] Can. 745, § 2, n. 2: "Adulti autem censentur, qui rationis usu fruuntur;

parents belongs to the Latin rite and the other is a member of an Oriental rite, the rite to which the father of the child belongs will be the determining factor to decide the rite of the child. If a child was baptized by a lay person, the child belongs to the rite of which the father is a member.[8]

a. *Baptized Persons*

A. Catholics

Persons who are members of the Catholic Church and are bound by the laws of the Church are subject to the law regarding the juridical form of marriage, unless they are exempt from the law by positive legislation.[9] If two Catholics who are certainly bound to observe the form of marriage attempt to contract a marriage either before a civil official or a non-Catholic minister, the marriage is null. Now, let it be supposed that this union proves to be an unhappy one, that after a few years the parties decide to separate and obtain a civil divorce or annulment, and that thereupon one of the parties wishes to marry a person in accordance with the laws of the Church. Before this party will be allowed to contract the proposed marriage, a declaration of nullity of the first marriage must be obtained from the competent ecclesiastical authority. The party must personally petition the ecclesiastical authority for this decree of nullity, even though the party was the cause of the nullity of the marriage. If the party can show to the satisfaction of the competent superior that he or she is free to marry, then the party establishes the right to marry. The party may have contracted the first marriage with the full knowledge that the marriage thus contracted was null, but this does not prevent or impede him or her from petitioning for a declaration of nullity. It is true that the person has committed a grave wrong and lived in sin, by associating with the other party in a

idque satis est ut suo quisque animi motu baptismum petat et ad illum admittatur." Cf. Cappello, *op. cit.,* I, n. 205.

[8] Can. 756, § 2: "Si alter parentum pertineat ad ritum latinum, alter ad orientalem, proles ritu patris baptizetur, nisi aliud iure speciali cautum sit." Cf. Cappello, *loc. cit.*; Vermeersch-Creusen, *Epitome Iuris Canonici* (3 vols., Vol. I, 6. ed., 1937; Vols. II-III, 5. ed., 1934-1936), I, n. 220.

[9] Cf. can. 1099.

null and void marriage, but that does not affect the juridical status of the person.

Catholics who knowingly and willingly contract or attempt to contract a marriage before a non-Catholic minister incur an excommunication according to the decrees of the III Plenary Council of Baltimore.[10] Since an excommunication is always a censure and never a vindictive penalty,[11] the party has a right to be absolved if he is truly sorry for the wrong he committed. Before a Catholic should be allowed to petition for a declaration of nullity, he should be questioned concerning the excommunication in order that it may be determined whether he really incurred it, and whether absolution from it has already been received. If the person was fully aware of the enacted censure of excommunication and knew that he or she would incur it by attempting to contract a marriage before a non-Catholic minister, then absolution from the censure must be given to the repentant person if no absolution has been previously bestowed.

In some dioceses, for example, Catholics who attempt to contract a mere civil marriage incur an excommunication. Before they may be allowed to petition for a declaration of nullity, they too should be absolved from the censure.

B. Non-Catholics

Anyone who has received baptism in a church other than the Catholic Church must be considered a non-Catholic. When a Catholic who is certainly subject to the form of marriage marries a baptized non-Catholic, either before a civil official or a non-Catholic minister, the marriage is null because of defect of form. The non-Catholic under these circumstances is also bound to observe the form of marriage because of the principle: *Pars ligata communicat alteri suum ligamen*. Let it now be supposed that this union proves to be unsuccessful, and that after a few years the parties decide to separate and obtain a civil divorce or annulment. In the meantime the non-Catholic party has become a convert to the Catholic Faith, and now wishes to marry a Catholic. The convert party must petition the competent authority for a declaration of nullity of the attempted mar-

[10] *Acta et Decreta Plenarii Baltimorensis Tertii* (Baltimorae: Typis Joannis Murphy et Sociorum, 1886), n. 127.

[11] Can. 2255, § 2: ". . . excommunicatio est semper censura . . ."

riage. But in the supposition that the baptized non-Catholic has not become a convert to the Catholic Faith, but now wishes to contract a new marriage with a third person, there is then the possibility that this third person is either a Catholic or a non-Catholic. In the latter instance it would be altogether unusual for a petition of the declaration of nullity to arise, for inasmuch as the parties of the proposed marriage are non-Catholics they would in all likelihood consider the granted civil divorce as sufficient for establishing a free status for the marriage. But if the divorced non-Catholic wishes to marry a Catholic, then the prenuptial investigation will reveal the fact of the non-Catholic's earlier attempted marriage. Is a decree of nullity required to establish the free status for the marriage on the part of the non-Catholic party? Who has the right to petition for the decree? A declaration of nullity is certainly required, for only the Church has a right to pass on the validity or nullity of a marriage in which a Catholic party was involved. Besides, the Church has a right to forbid the prospective marriage, involving a Catholic, until it has passed on the freedom of both parties to contract it. But as regards the one who must sign the petition for the decree, it must be kept in mind that the declaration of nullity is not a judicial process which excludes non-Catholics from acting as plaintiffs in matrimonial cases,[12] and therefore the rules of the judicial process cannot be applied here. The declaration of nullity simply states that a marriage is null by reason of lack of form. In other words, it establishes in an administrative manner the fact that the person involved in the case is free to marry. But baptized non-Catholics have a right to marry, if they can show that they are free. Nowhere does the law forbid them to petition for the opportunity to offer proof of their freedom. Therefore, the baptized non-Catholic is not barred in any way from petitioning the competent superior for a decree of nullity, in order to establish that he or she is free to contract a marriage in accordance with the laws of the Church. This case may become practical when the address of the Catholic party of the first union in the case cannot be ascertained, or when the address is known but the Catholic party cannot be reached, or when the Catholic party has become insane in the meantime or refuses to enter a petition. But

[12] Cf. 1936 Instruction, Art. 35, § 3.

even apart from these circumstances the superior can issue a decree of nullity at the request of the non-Catholic party in the case. However, the emergence of all scandal must be avoided. The non-Catholic party must be instructed that the Church is not granting a divorce or an annulment of a marriage, but is merely declaring that a marriage never existed between the Catholic and the baptized non-Catholic, because the first marriage was contracted contrary to the prescriptions of the Church.

It may be asked whether the Church has a duty or obligation to issue a decree of nullity, thereby enabling the non-Catholic party to contract a new marriage according to the prescriptions of the law? The solution to this problem is not to be sought in the fact that the Church cannot prevent capable and free parties to contract a marriage, unless there exists an impediment of either the divine or the ecclesiastical law between the parties who seek to contract a marriage. For according to the present constitution of the law, a person who attempts to contract a marriage in contravention of the law concerning the juridical form of marriage, does not thereby contract an impediment of either the divine or the ecclesiastical law. The marriage thus attempted simply does not exist, and hence the person is free to marry. A declaration of nullity is not a dispensation from an impediment; it is merely an authentic document testifying to the fact that the attempted marriage was null by reason of lack of form. It is true that the competent authority, after having made the necessary investigation in an administrative process, and being convinced of the evident nullity of the marriage, certainly could not impede a person from contracting a new marriage in accordance with the norms of the law, for in impeding a person from contracting a new marriage, the competent authority would be establishing a new impediment. This is certainly beyond the powers of ordinaries or pastors. However, if there existed a grave danger for the arising of scandal if a decree of nullity were granted, the competent superior could prevent the party from contracting a new marriage for a certain length of time until that danger of scandal is no longer present.

The solution of the problem whether the Church has a duty or obligation to issue a decree of nullity to non-Catholics must be sought in the words of canon 87 which states that by baptism a person becomes a subject of the Church of Christ with all the rights and duties of a Christian, unless, in so far as rights are concerned, there is some obstacle impeding the bond of communion with the Church, or a censure inflicted by the Church.[13] Therefore, the Church does not have an obligation or duty to issue a decree of nullity to a non-Catholic party. In cases of non-Catholics there certainly exists an obstacle which impedes the bond of communion with the Church.

However, in a private response of the Holy Office of April 20, 1931,[14] to the Bishop of Harrisburg, it is stated that a non-Catholic party is not excluded from the part of a plaintiff in the summary process under canon 1990.[15] If a non-Catholic party is not excluded from the part of a plaintiff in a summary process, he or she is certainly not excluded from the part of a petitioner in an administrative process.

[13] Can. 87: "Baptismate homo constituitur in Ecclesia Christi persona cum omnibus christianorum iuribus et officiis, nisi, ad iura quod attinet, obstet obex, ecclesiasticae communionis vinculum impediens, vel lata ab Ecclesia censura."

[14] Bouscaren, *The Canon Law Digest,* II, 267, under can. 1990.

[15] The following question was referred to the Holy Office by the Most Reverend Bishop of Harrisburg:

Rebecca, an unbaptized person, contracted marriage with Allen, a baptized non-Catholic, on 8 Apr., 1917.

On 8 Nov., 1926, Rebecca obtained a civil divorce on grounds of desertion and cruelty.

Rebecca now seeks a declaration of nullity of her marriage on the ground that at the time of the marriage the impediment of disparity of cult existed.

Since, however, according to the decision of the Holy Office, of 27 Jan., 1928, diocesan Curias are declared incompetent to adjudicate cases of this kind because of the incapacity of the parties thereto, I, Bishop of Harrisburg, refer this case to the aforesaid Sacred Congregation of the Holy Office.

The reason for asking an ecclesiastical declaration of nullity is this: to enable Rebecca to contract marriage before the Church, with Henry, a Catholic.

Authentic documents for the proof of the allegations are retained in our Archives for safety's sake.

Reply. The Holy Office, on 20 Apr., 1931, sent the following reply: After careful consideration, this Supreme Sacred Congregation decided to reply, that the aforesaid case can be handled by the Ordinary himself according to canons 1990-1992.

The prescriptions of the aforesaid canons are to be observed exactly and in their entirety in deciding the matter, both as regards the certainty of the existence of the impediment and of the fact that no dispensation from it has

C. Apostates

A section of Article 231 of the Instruction reads as follows: " . . . aut si apostatae a fide catholica in apostasia civiliter vel ritu alieno se iunxerunt. . . . " According to Mörsdorf [16] this sentence seems to be entirely superfluous, because, it is already contained in the first section of the same article, which states: "Si quis certo tenebatur ad canonicam formam celebrationis matrimonii et tantum civile matrimonium contraxit, vel coram ministro acatholico matrimonium inivit. . . . " Furthermore, in the opinion of Mörsdorf, the above cited section is not quite to the point, because if a person is born of a mixed marriage, baptized in the Catholic Church, but reared in infidelity, because the Catholic parent apostatized soon after the baptism of the child, the child is not bound to observe the form for the celebration of the marriage, when contracting a marriage with a non-Catholic.[17] Therefore, Mörsdorf concludes, if the offspring is not bound to observe the form of marriage, the marriage cannot be declared null because of defect of form. The apostasy of the Catholic parent does not affect the child in regard to the juridical form of marriage, as long as the prescriptions of canon 1099, § 2, are verified, according to which the child is exempt from the obligation to observe the juridical form of marriage. However, if someone is certainly bound to observe the form of marriage, then no matter if the person himself apostatized or not, such a person is subject to the juridical form, and therefore is already included in the first section of Article 231. Even if the parents, both of whom are Catholics, apostatized after the birth of the child and after having had the child baptized in the Catholic Church, the person is bound to observe

been obtained, and as regards the procedure. If the matter is doubtful, it should be referred to the Holy Office.

When the invalidity of the marriage shall have been proved with certainty according to this procedure, Your Excellency may apply to this Sacred Congregation for a dispensation from the impediment of disparity of cult, giving the reasons which support it, and having obtained in advance the *cautiones* which are required according to canon 1061, so that a new marriage may be contracted with a Catholic man.—Bouscaren, *loc. cit.*

[16] "Zur Eheprozessordnung für die Diözesangerichte vom 15. August 1936," —*Theol. Quartalschrift,* CXX (1939), 216.

[17] Can. 1099.

the form, because it cannot be included in the exemption of canon 1099, and therefore, the person is already included in the first section of the above quoted article.[18]

It seems that Mörsdorf failed to understand the true meaning of the phrase " . . . aut si apostatae a fide catholica in apostasia civiliter vel ritu alieno se iunxerunt. . . ." The whole Article 231 presumes that a person knows that he or she is bound to observe the juridical form of matrimony. The apostates are given the benefit of the doubt. It is hoped that the apostates will return to the Faith, if they inquire about the nullity of the marriage which was contracted by them outside the Church. The Church is willing to lift the obstacle, if the apostate disregarded the law concerning the juridical form of matrimony. Heretics are usually not concerned about the nullity of the marriage contracted outside the Church, and Article 231 does not mention them expressly, whereas Article 231 adds an explicit rule concerning apostates, namely: " . . . aut si apostatae a fide catholica in apostasia civiliter vel ritu alieno se iunxerunt. . . . "

The question may arise whether the apostate party is allowed to petition the competent authority for a decree of nullity because of lack of form in his attempted marriage. The same must be said here what has been said before concerning non-Catholics.[19] Therefore, let it be supposed that the apostate, who was certainly bound to observe the form of marriage, attempts to contract a marriage with a baptized non-Catholic before a civil official or non-Catholic minister. After a few years the parties decide to separate and obtain a civil divorce. The apostate, who now desires to marry a Catholic, admits in the prenuptial investigation that he was married before to a non-Catholic. A declaration of nullity is necessary.

b. *Non-baptized Persons*

Non-baptized persons are those who have not received baptism in any religious denomination; or those who have received baptism, but whose baptism is certainly invalid. While non-baptized persons do not fall within the scope of purely ecclesiastical laws, they must observe the requirements of the form of marriage when they contract

[18] Cf. *infra,* Chap. IV, n. 2.

[19] Cf. *supra,* pp. 34, 35.

a marriage with one who is certainly bound to observe the form because of the principle: *Pars ligata communicat alteri suum ligamen.* If, therefore, a non-baptized person marries a Catholic either before a civil official or a non-Catholic minister, the marriage is both null by reason of defect of form and invalid by virtue of the impediment of disparity of worship,[20] provided that the parties did not obtain a dispensation from the diriment impediment. Let it be supposed that this marriage is unsuccessful, and that the parties decide to obtain a civil divorce or an annulment. The non-baptized party meets a Catholic, and wishes to marry the Catholic in accordance with the necessary dispensation from the impediment of disparity of worship. During the course of the prenuptial investigation the fact of the former marriage with a Catholic before a civil official or a non-Catholic minister is revealed. A closer investigation into the case discloses that the Catholic party has already obtained a decree of nullity of the so-called marriage with the non-baptized person. As long as a certified copy of this decree can be obtained, and the non-baptized person can establish his or her identity so as to exclude all danger of fraud and deception, a new decree of nullity is not required. But if upon closer investigation into the case it is shown that the marriage was indeed null, but no decree of nullity has yet been granted, the non-baptized party must petition the ecclesiastical authority for a declaration of nullity. This follows the same principles that have been explained in regard to non-Catholics.[21]

2. Members of the Oriental Rite

Members of the Oriental Church, with the exception of the Ruthenians,[22] are *per se* not bound to observe the form of marriage,[23]

[20] Can. 1099 and can. 1070.

[21] Cf. *supra*, pp. 34, 35.

[22] They call themselves Ukrainians. Historically this is the far less noble and significant name of the two. *Ukraine* simply means "the borderland" or "marches." However, so far as the Catholics are concerned, "Ruthenian" is still their official ecclesiastical designation. Cf. Attwater, *The Catholic Eastern Churches* (Revised edition, Milwaukee: The Bruce Publishing Company, 1937), p. 76.

[23] Cf. *infra*, Chap. IV.

provided that they contract a marriage among themselves or with heretics or schismatics. If a member of an Oriental rite marries a member of the Latin rite, who is certainly bound to observe the form of marriage, the marriage is null if this marriage was contracted either civilly or before a non-Catholic minister. If they separate after a while, and the member of the Oriental rite wishes to contract a marriage with a member of the Latin rite, he or she must obtain a decree of nullity from the Latin ecclesiastical superior. But if he or she wants to marry a member of an Oriental rite, the case must be referred to the Sacred Congregation for the Oriental Church.

But if two Ruthenians, who are bound to observe the form of marriage,[24] contract a marriage before a civil official or non-Catholic minister, they must obtain a decree of nullity from their own ordinary. It is customary that the ordinaries for the Ruthenian Catholics, one for the Podcarpathians and the other for the Galicians, in this country grant a decree of nullity, if the Ruthenians neglected to observe the form of marriage. The case must be referred to the respective ordinary of the Ruthenian Catholics before the parties may be allowed to contract a new marriage.[25]

3. The Parties in a Case of Doubt

Whenever there exists the appearance or semblance of a marriage, whenever there exists a prudent doubt, the rules of judicial procedure must be followed if the validity of the marriage is questioned.[26] But inasmuch as the judicial process must be followed, the parties involved in the case must be treated accordingly.

The ordinary trial is a judicial process and hence a case can never be introduced by the tribunal *ex officio,* but a case must be introduced in the form of an accusation either by one party or both or by the

[24] Cf. *infra,* Chap. IV.

[25] One of the ordinaries resides in Philadelphia, Pa., and the other in Homestead, Pa. The above information was received from the Chancery Office of the ordinary for the Ruthenian Catholics, Philadelphia, Pa., through the courtesy of the Superior of the St. Josaphat Seminary, Washington, D. C.

[26] Cf. Art. 231, § 2; cf. also *infra,* Chap. VII.

promoter of justice. The ones who have a right to impugn the marriage are primarily the parties themselves, unless they have been the direct cause of the impediment.[27]

The term *impediment* must be understood in its widest sense and hence it includes not only the impediments strictly so-called but also lack of consent and lack of form. This is evident from an answer of the Pontifical Commission to the question: "Whether the word *impediment* in canon 1971, § 1, n. 1, is to be understood as applying only to impediments strictly so-called (cans. 1067-1080), or also to impediments improperly so-called which invalidate marriage (cans. 1081-1103). To this query the Pontifical Commission of Interpretation replied: In the negative to the first part; in the affirmative to the second." [28] Therefore, if the parties were the cause of the lack of form, they are thereby incapable of impugning their marriage.

The Pontifical Commission was asked: "Whether, according to canon 1971, § 1, n. 1, the party who was the culpable cause of the impediment or of the nullity of the marriage has also the right to impugn it. To this question the Pontifical Commission replied in the negative." [29]

However, in order to be incapable of impugning the marriage, it is not sufficient that the party simply be the cause of the impediment, but that the party be the culpable and direct cause of the im-

[27] Can. 1971, § 1, n. 1: "Habiles ad accusandum sunt: Coniuges, in omnibus causis separationis et nullitatis, nisi ipsi fuerint impedimenti causa." Cf. 1936 Instruction, Art. 35, § 1, n. 1: "Habiles ad accusandum sunt: Coniuges, nisi ipsi fuerint impedimenti causa."

[28] Pont. Comm. Intr., 12 mart. 1929: "D.—Utrum vox *impedimenti* canonis 1971, § 1, n. 1, intelligenda sit tantum de impedimentis proprie dictis (can. 1067-1080), an etiam de impedimentis improprie dictis matrimonium dirimentibus (can. 1081-1103). R.—Negative ad primam partem, affirmative ad secundam."—*AAS,* XXI (1929), 171; for English translation, cf. Bouscaren, *The Canon Law Digest,* I, 807, under can. 1971. Cf. also Haring, "Das Klagerecht im kanonischen Eheprozess,"—*AKKR,* CXV (1935), 111.

[29] Pont. Comm. Intr., 17 iul. 1933: "D.—II. An, ad normam eiusdem canonis 1971, § 1, n. 1, habilis sit ad accusandum matrimonium etiam coniux, qui fuerit causa culpabilis sive impedimenti sive nullitatis matrimonii. R.—Ad II. Negative."—*AAS,* XXV (1933), 345; for English translation, cf. Bouscaren, *op. cit.,* I, 808, under can. 1971.

pediment. Any person who is the *causa impedimenti vel nullitatis matrimonii* in any other way than through a combination both of direct action and of deliberative intent would not be barred from presenting to an ecclesiastical court his plea regarding the nullity of his marriage.[80]

Briefly, the right to impugn the marriage is lost only by the party who was the culpable and direct cause of the impediment. If both parties are the culpable and direct causes of the impediment or the nullity, neither of them will be capable of impugning the marriage; however, they may denounce the nullity of the marriage to the ordinary or to the promoter of justice, for the Pontifical Commission answered the following question in the affirmative: "Whether the parties to a marriage, who according to canon 1971, § 1, n. 1, and the interpretation of March 12, 1929, are incapable of being petitioners to have the marriage declared invalid, have at least in virtue of paragraph 2 of the same canon, 1971, the right to notify the ordinary or the promoter of justice of the nullity of the marriage." [81] But, it must be noted, the promoter of justice can enter court proceedings only *propter bonum publicum,* and not for the benefit of a private individual who wants to contract another marriage.

All other persons, even though they be blood relatives of the consorts, have not the right to impugn the marriage, but only to denounce the nullity of the marriage to the ordinary or promoter of justice.[82] The promoter of justice, by his own right, even without

[80] "D. Utrum, secundum canonem 1971, § 1, n. 1, et responsum diei 17 iulii 1933 ad II, inhabilis ad accusandum matrimonium habendus sit tantum coniux, qui sive impedimenti sive nullitatis matrimonii causa fuit et directa et dolosa, an etiam coniux qui impedimenti vel nullitatis matrimonii causa exstitit vel indirecta vel doli expers. R. Affirmative ad primam partem, negative ad secundam."—27 iulii 1942—*The Jurist,* III (1943), 156.

[81] Pont. Comm. Intr., 17 febr. 1930: "D.—An coniuges qui, iuxta canonem 1971; § 1, n. 1, et interpretationem diei 12 martii 1929, habiles non sunt ad accusandum matrimonium, vi eiusdem canonis 2 ius saltem habeant nullitatem matrimonii Ordinario vel promotori iustitiae denuntiandi. R.—Affirmative."—*AAS,* XXII (1930), 196; for English translation, cf. Bouscaren, *op. cit.,* I, 888, under can. 1971.

[82] Art. 35, § 2: "Reliqui omnes, etsi consanguinei, non habent ius accusandi matrimonium, sed tantum nullitatem matrimonii Ordinario vel promotori iustitiae denuntiandi." Cf. can. 1971.

previous denunciation, is capable of impugning the marriage provided that the impediments which cause the invalidity of the marriage are of their nature public.[83]

It is very much disputed as to what is meant by the expression *in impedimentis natura sua publicis.* It is the common opinion that an impediment of its very nature public is one that can be proved by public and authentic documents; such impediments are consanguinity, affinity, spiritual and legal relationship, holy orders, solemn religious profession, disparity of cult.[84] The curial practice goes even so far as to declare every cause for nullity by its very nature public.[85] Köstler [86] defends the opinion that the impediments of their very nature public, which entitle the promoter of justice to impugn the marriage, are none other than the impediments of public interest (*impedimenta iuris publici*). He claims that the phrase "of its nature public" does not mean anything else than that which touches public interest.

Inasmuch as the promoter of justice may impugn the marriage only if the impediments are public of their very nature, it seems that the question of the nullity of a marriage because of lack of form cannot be included here, just as the lack of consent is not included.[87] If lack of form or lack of consent were included, the party who was the culpable and direct cause of the nullity of the marriage could easily denounce the marriage to the promoter of justice, and thus reach his end.

[83] Can. 1971, § 1, n. 2: "Habiles ad accusandum sunt: . . . Promotor iustitiae in impedimentis natura sua publicis." Cf. Art. 35, § 1, n. 2: "Habiles ad accusandum sunt: . . . Promotor iustitiae, in impedimentis natura sua publicis, iure proprio et absque praevia denunciatione . . ."

[84] Chelodi, *Ius Matrimoniale iuxta Codicem Iuris Canonici* (4. ed., recognita et aucta a Vigilio Dalpiaz, Tridenti: Libreria Moderna Editrice A. Ardesi, 1937), p. 35; Jone, *Gesetzbuch des kanonischen Rechtes* (3 vols., Paderborn: Ferdinand Schöningh, 1939-1941), II, 226-227; Triebs, *Handbuch des kanonischen Eherechts*, p. 145.

[85] Mocnik, "Das Klagerecht des *Promotor iustitiae* bei *vis et metus*,"—*Theol.-prakt. Quartalschrift*, LXXXVII (1934), 149; Haring, "Fälle aus der Ehegerichtspraxis,"—*Theol.-prakt. Quartalschrift*, LXXXIX (1936), 356.

[86] *Das österreichische Konkordats-Eherecht* (Wien: Julius Springer, 1937), p. 32.

[87] Hollnsteiner, *Die Sprachpraxis der S. Romana Rota in Ehenichtigkeitsprozessen seit Geltung des C. I. C.* (Freiburg: Herder, 1934), p. 48.

It is quite evident that non-Catholics may not act as plaintiffs in marriage cases, even though the marriage is null by reason of lack of form, when the form was vitiated by reason of some substantial defect.[88] If both parties in the case are non-Catholics, they must receive permission from the Holy Office to impugn the marriage; and in particular cases, one of the non-Catholic parties may get permission from the Holy Office to impugn the marriage.[89]

[88] Cf. *infra,* Chap. VII.

[89] 1936 Instruction, Art. 35, § 3: "Itidem actoris partes agere nequeunt in causis matrimonialibus acatholici sive baptizati sive non baptizati; si quidem autem speciales occurrant rationes ad eosdem admittendos, recurrendum est in singulis casibus ad S. C. S. Officii." Cf. also S. C. S. Off., 27 maii 1928: "I.—Utrum in causis matrimonialibus acatholicus, sive baptizatus sive non baptizatus, actoris partes agere possit . . ." R.—Ad I. Negative, seu standum Codici I. C., praesertim canoni 87. Si quidem autem speciales occurrant rationes ad admittendos acatholicos ut actores in huiusmodi causis, recurrendum ad S. S. Congregationem S. Officii in singulis casibus . . ."—*AAS,* XX (1928), 75; cf. Hilling, "Eine Entscheidung des hl. Offiziums über die kirchliche Gerichtsbarkeit zweier akatholischen Eheleute,"—*AKKR,* CVII (1927), 569 ss. Cf. Haring, "Fälle aus der Ehegerichtspraxis,"—*Theol.-prakt. Quartalschrift,* LXXXIX (1936), 357.

CHAPTER IV

THE FORM OF MARRIAGE

THE first section of Article 231 of the Instruction briefly states: *Si quis certe tenebatur ad canonicam formam celebrationis matrimonii. . . .* This short sentence expresses a matter that has been treated by many authors.[1] But in order to present a complete picture of the declaration of nullity procedure, one must properly discuss the nature of the form of marriage, point out who is bound to observe it, and indicate who is exempt from the juridical form by positive legislation.

The internal consent of the parties must be manifested externally in a form prescribed by the Church. The parties must observe those solemnities which the Church prescribes for the contracting of a true and valid marriage.[2] The form of marriage consists in this that the parties exchange true matrimonial consent, and that the marriage ceremony is performed either by the pastor of the bride, who has prior rights to perform the marriage; or in the case of a just reason or in every case involving members of the Oriental rite, excluding the Ruthenians, by the pastor of the groom; or by the ordinary of the place; or by a priest delegated by either the competent pastor or by

[1] Cf. Payen, *De Matrimonio in Missionibus ac potissimum in Sinis* (Tractatus Practicus et Casus, Altera editio, 3 vols., Zi-ka-wei: In Typographia T'ou-se-we, 1936), II, 155-270; Chelodi, *Ius Matrimoniale,* pp. 158-180; Jone, *Gesetzbuch des kanonischen Rechts,* II, 306-324; Gasparri, *Tractatus Canonicus de Matrimonio* (editio nova ad mentem Codicis I. C., 2 vols., Romae: Typis Polyglottis Vaticanis, 1932), II, 101-161; Ayrinhac, *Marriage Legislation in the New Code of Canon Law* (New, revised edition, revised and enlarged by P. J. Lydon, New York, Boston, Cincinnati, Chicago, San Francisco: Benziger Brothers, Inc., 1941), pp. 234-275; Triebs, *Handbuch des kanonischen Eherechts,* pp. 557-637; Cappello, *Tractatus Canonico-Moralis de Sacramentis* (3 vols. in 6, Vol. III, *De Matrimonio,* editio quarta et aucta, Taurinorum Augustae: Officina Libraria Marietti, 1939), nn. 648-722; Carberry, *The Judicial Form of Marriage,* The Catholic University of America Canon Law Studies, n. 84 (Washington, D. C.: The Catholic University of America, 1934).

[2] Gasparri, *De Matrimonio,* n. 926.

the ordinary of the place. The marriage is valid, though not licit, if the priest assisting is not the pastor of the bride or groom, if he acts within his territory.[3]

It does not follow, however, that the priest is the minister of the sacrament of matrimony; the priest is merely the authorized witness of the Church, whereas the parties themselves are the ministers of the sacrament. If the priest were the minister of the sacrament, a marriage would never be contracted validly unless it were contracted in the presence and with the blessing of a priest. But under certain circumstances a marriage can be contracted validly even if the priest is not present to bless the marriage.[4]

Futhermore, the presence of two witnesses belongs to the essential requisites of the form of marriage. Aside from the fact that at least two persons must be present to witness the marriage, the Code does not lay down any other prescriptions as regards the qualifications of these witnesses. It is sufficient, therefore, that the witnesses are aware of the identity of the parties concerned and of the fact that these parties are contracting a marriage, so that they are able to testify later, if called upon, that these parties manifested their consent externally.[5] Hence, the witnesses must be present physically; but it is not necessary that they hear the affirmative answers given by the parties in response to the priest's query, as long as they are

[3] Can. 1094: "Ea tantum matrimonia valida sunt quae contrahuntur coram parocho, vel loci Ordinario, vel sacerdote ab alterutro delegato et duobus saltem testibus, secundum tamen regulas expressas in canonibus qui sequuntur, et salvis exceptionibus de quibus in can. 1098, 1099." Cf. can. 1097, § 2: "In quolibet casu pro regula habeatur ut matrimonium coram sponsae parocho celebretur, nisi iusta causa excuset; matrimonia autem catholicorum mixti ritus, nisi aliud particulari iure cautum sit, in ritu viri et coram eiusdem parocho sunt celebranda." As regards the Ruthenians, cf. S. C. pro Ecclesia Orientali, decr. *"Cum data fuerit,"* 1 mart. 1929, Art. 39: "Matrimonia tum inter fideles graeco-ruthenos, tum inter fideles mixti ritus, servata forma decreti 'Ne temere' contrahi debent, ac proinde in ritu mulieris a parocho mulieris benedicenda sunt."—*AAS*, XXI (1929), 152. The following was added to Article 39 in 1940: "Quod si iusta causa adsit, proterunt nuptiae celebrari in ritu viri, de iudicio et consensu Ordinarii loci."—*AAS*, XXXIII (1941), 27; cf. also *The Jurist*, I (1941), 267.

[4] Can. 1098. Cf. Hervé, *Manuale Theologiae Dogmaticae*, IV, 534, n. 482b.

[5] Gasparri, *op. cit.*, n. 961; Jone, *Gesetzbuch des kanoniscken Rechts*, II, 307-308.

aware of the fact that from the external signs it is evident that the parties contract the marriage.

Two men or two women or one man and one woman may act as witnesses. It is immaterial whether the witnesses are relatives of the parties, minors, infidels or excommunicated persons. However, the Holy Office on August 19, 1891, declared that infidels or heretics should not be called upon to act as witnesses at a marriage, but that they may be tolerated by the ordinary of the place for a just reason, and provided that no scandal will arise from this toleration.[6]

The marriage is not rendered invalid if the persons were forced to act as witnesses, or through deceit were induced to witness this marriage. The right to appoint witnesses does not belong to the pastor, but belongs entirely to the parties themselves, unless the parties fail to make an appointment.[7]

Therefore, the essential requisities for a valid form of marriage are the presence of at least five persons:

a. The parties themselves or their proxies; [8]

b. The competent pastor of the bride or the groom, as the case may be; for validity, a pastor acting within his territory; the local ordinary; or a priest delegated by either the pastor or the ordinary;

c. Two witnesses.

If any of these requisites is lacking the marriage is invalid by reason of defect of form. It is true that in these cases where only some element is lacking, there exists at least the appearance of a true marriage; but the validity of the marriage is vitiated because of a substantial defect in the canonical form. Therefore, these cases are different from the cases of complete lack of form, when the parties attempt a marriage either civilly or before a non-Catholic minister; and these cases cannot be handled in an administrative process.[9]

By positive ecclesiastical legislation certain parties are exempt from the observance of the required form of marriage, as this is provided for in canon 1099, § 2, which exempts non-Catholics who

[6] Cf. *Fontes,* n. 1144.

[7] Jone, *op. cit.,* II, 308.

[8] Can. 1088, § 1: "Ad matrimonium valide contrahendum necesse est ut contrahentes sint praesentes sive per se ipsi sive per procuratorem."

[9] Cf. *infra,* Chap. VII.

contract a marriage among themselves, irrespective of the previous reception or non-reception of baptism by them. The children of non-Catholic parents, if these children were baptized in the Catholic Church but brought up in heresy or schism from infancy on, are also exempt from the juridical form of marriage, if they enter into a marriage with a non-Catholic.[10]

Another exemption by positive legislation is present in a case of necessity wherein the parties foresee that for the next thirty days it is physically or morally impossible for them to go to a priest or for a priest to come to them.[11]

1. Who Is Bound to Observe the Form?

A person is incorporated into the membership of the Church of Christ through the valid reception of baptism.[12] This incorporation implies that a person assumes all rights and obligations of a Christian. It follows, therefore, that the non-baptized person has neither rights nor obligations in the Church. Thus, the non-baptized person is not

[10] Can. 1099, § 2: "Firmo autem praescripto 1, n. 1, acatholici sive baptizati sive non baptizati, si inter se contrahant, nullibi tenentur ad catholicam matrimonii formam servandam; item ab acatholicis nati, etsi in Ecclesia catholica baptizati, qui ab infantili aetate in haeresi vel schismate aut infidelitate vel sine ulla religione adoleverunt, quoties cum parte acatholica contraxerint."

[11] Can. 1098: "Si haberi vel adiri nequeat sine gravi incommodo parochus vel Ordinarius vel sacerdos delegatus qui matrimonio assistant ad normam canonum 1095, 1096: 1°. In mortis periculo validum et licitum est matrimonium contractum coram solis testibus; et etiam extra mortis periculum, dummodo prudenter praevideatur eam rerum conditionem esse per mensem duraturam; 2°. In utroque casu, si praesto sit alius sacerdos qui adesse possit, vocari et, una cum testibus, matrimonio assistere debet, salva coniugii validitate coram solis testibus." Cf. Pont. Comm. Intr., 25 iulii 1931: D.—An *ad physicam parochi vel Ordinarii loci absentiam,* de qua in interpretatione diei 10 martii 1928 ad canonem 1098, referendus sit etiam casus, quo parochus vel Ordinarius, licet materialiter praesens in loco, ob grave tamen incommodum celebrationi matrimonii assistere nequeat, requirens et excipiens contrahentium consensum. R.—Affirmative." Cf. also Hannan, "Informal Marriage,"—*The Jurist,* III (1943), 149-151.

[12] Can. 87: "Baptismate homo constituitur in Ecclesia Christi persona cum omnibus christianorum iuribus et officiis, nisi, ad iura quod attinet, obstet obex, ecclesiasticae communionis vinculum impediens, vel lata ab Ecclesia censura."

subject to the ecclesiastical laws, if these laws are of purely ecclesiastical origin. This is expressed in the Code, when it states that as far as the subject of law is concerned, the non-baptized do not fall under those laws which are purely ecclesiastical.[13]

The fact that a person is baptized and is thus made a subject of the law by no means indicates that this person may exercise all the rights which the law accords. Heretics and schismatics, for example, although they are baptized, are denied the free exercise of their rights, because they do not acknowledge the divine authority of the Church, and they are under excommunication *speciali modo* reserved to the Holy See.[14] Baptized persons who have incurred a censure are deprived of the free exercise of their rights, either partially or totally.[15] But all baptized persons, whether they acknowledge or reject the divine authority of the Church, are bound by the obligations which they assume in baptism.[16] It is quite evident that a denial of authority does not release one from the obligations one has in relation to that authority. Whether the authority be civil or ecclesiactical is immaterial.[17]

It is true that a person may relinquish his citizenship in a particular country, or he may lose it, and then he is free from all obligations toward this particular civil government. On the contrary, a person once baptized can never dissolve his membership in the Church of Christ, for according to the will of Christ baptism imprints an indelible mark on the soul of the recipient and is a regeneration to supernatural life. Just as a man in natural birth becomes the member of a particular family, and thus contracts a bond that can never be severed, so also through the valid reception of baptism, the supernatural birth, man becomes a member of the Church, thus contracting a relationship that can never be broken. The Church under certain conditions can exempt persons from certain obligations. The

[13] Can. 12: "Legibus mere ecclesiasticis non tenentur qui baptismum non receperunt, nec baptizati qui sufficienti rationis usu non gaudent, nec qui, licet rationis usum assecuti, septimum aetatis annum nondum expleverunt, nisi aliud iure expresse caveatur."

[14] Cf. can. 87; can. 2314.

[15] Cf. can. 87; can. 2241.

[16] Cf. can. 87.

[17] Triebs, *Handbuch des kanonischen Eherechts*, p. 605.

reason and the extent of such exemptions are different under different circumstances.

All Catholics are bound to observe the prescribed juridical form for the celebration of matrimony whenever they contract marriage among themselves.[18] The term *Catholic* embraces those who were baptized in the Catholic Church in infancy as well as those who were converted to the Catholic Faith. It must be noted that the validity of the baptism is not questioned, because the validity of the baptism is presupposed. But once baptism has been conferred, the question arises: To what Christian community does the baptized person belong as a member? In other words, in what Christian faith does this baptized person hold communion? The deciding factor in the solution of this question does not rest with the fact that baptism has been conferred, or with the rite which may have been followed in the administration of baptism; the deciding factor is constituted either by the intention of the person baptized, if he was an adult and thus was capable of forming an intention, or by the intention of the parents or guardians, or, in the absence of both parents and guardians, by the intention of the one baptizing, whether he functioned as the ordinary or as an extraordinary minister of the sacrament of baptism.

A conflict of intentions between the baptized adult and the person baptizing is hardly conceivable, unless it happens through error, and then the intention of the one baptized prevails. But a conflict of intentions may exist between the parents or guardians of the person baptized on the one hand, and the one who conferred the baptism on the other hand. In those cases the intention of the parents or guardians will prevail over the intention of the minister. The parents decide to which religion the child should belong. Normally and ordinarily it is to be presumed that the parents have the intention that the child be baptized and become a member of that religious faith of which they themselves are members. It does not make any difference whether this intention is actually expressed or reasonably presumed.[19]

[18] Can. 1099, § 1, n. 1: "Ad statutam superius formam servandam tenentur: Omnes in catholica Ecclesia baptizati et ad eam ex haeresi aut schismate conversi, licet sive hi sive illi ab eadem postea defecerint, quoties inter se matrimonium ineunt. . . ."

[19] Hilling, "Neueste Entscheidungen des Hl. Stuhles über das Ehehindernis

If a child is born of Catholic parents, but is baptized by the attending physician who has the intention to baptize it in some heretical sect, the child must nevertheless be considered as having been baptized *in Ecclesia catholica,* for one can reasonably presume that that was the intention of the Catholic parents, which intention prevails over that of the attending physician. There are certain exceptional cases in which the Catholic parents present their child to a non-Catholic minister for baptism with the full intention to have the child baptized in the heretical sect and to make it a member of that sect. That those cases exist is evident from the fact that the Church found it necessary to decree a punishment against the parents guilty of such a crime.[20]

If the intention of the parents is doubtful or cannot be ascertained, as may happen in cases in which the parents do not belong to any particular religious faith, or in the cases of foundling, then the intention of the one baptizing is the deciding factor, provided that the person baptized has not as yet reached the use of reason which makes it possible for him to form his own intention. If the intention of the minister is decisive, the presumption is that the minister wishes to baptize the person in and make it a member of that religious faith to which he himself belongs. If the minister, ordinary or extraordinary, of baptism is a Catholic, then the person baptized is considered to be baptized *in Ecclesia catholica.*

It may happen that the one baptizing just wishes to make the child a Christian without aggregating it to any one particular religious denomination. In a case of this kind the child would be considered as baptized *in Ecclesia catholica,* for it is the doctrine of the Church that the Church founded by Jesus Christ and the Catholic Church are one and the same. If a Jewish physician, for example, baptizes a foundling with the intention to make the child a Christian, but not a member of any particular religious denomination, the child must be considered as baptized *in Ecclesia catholica.*[21]

der Religionsverschiedenheit, die Auflösung einer Naturehe und die Anwendung des Privilegium Paulinum,"—*AKKR,* CVII (1927), 181.

[20] Can. 2319, § 1, n. 3: "Subsunt excommunicationi latae sententiae Ordinario reservatae catholici: Qui scienter liberos suos acatholicis ministris baptizandos offerre praesumunt."

[21] Jone, *Gesetzbuch des kanonischen Rechts,* II, 266; Gasparri, *De Matri-*

According to the terminology of canon 1099, § 1, only those who are baptized *in Ecclesia catholica* are bound to observe the form of marriage. In reality this canon constitutes an exception to canon 87, according to which canon all baptized persons are subject to the ecclesiastical laws.

The conversion to the Catholic Faith from heresy or schism can be brought about either expressly, that is, through a formal act, or tacitly, that is, through actions from which one can prudently judge that the person wishes to be considered a convert to the Catholic Faith, provided that the baptism, which was conferred in heresy or schism, was administered validly. A person, for example, is born of non-Catholic parents and baptized validly by a non-Catholic minister. But the person is instructed in the Catholic Faith from early youth on, inasmuch as the parents became converts to the Catholic Faith before the child had reached the use of reason. This child must be considered a convert, even though it personally was never converted, because it always knowingly and willingly belonged to the Catholic Church.[22] Of course, the validity of the baptism must be determined

monio, nn. 568 ss. The fact whether or not a person is baptized *in Ecclesia catholica* is important for the question of the impediment of disparity of worship. Since only those persons are exempt from the diriment impediment who have received baptism outside the Catholic Church, a person baptized *in Ecclesia catholica* is bound by the impediment, even though he was born of non-Catholic parents, and reared in heresy, schism or infidelity from infancy. This can be authentically substantiated by the following: Pont. Comm. Intr., 29 apr. 1940: "Whether the persons born of non-Catholics, mentioned in canon 1099, § 2, are bound, according to canon 1070, by the impediment of disparity of cult when they contract marriage with an unbaptized person. Reply: In the affirmative."—*AAS,* XXXII (1940), 312. Cf. Bouscaren, *Supplement—1941,* p. 128, under canon 1070.

[22] S. R. R., *Nullitatis matrimonii,* 9 aug. 1926, *coram R. P. D. Francisco Parrillo,* dec. XXXIX, n. 4: "Prout planum est, sub nomine catholicorum, qui inductam formam servandam adstringuntur, veniunt sive ii, qui in Ecclesia catholica baptismum receperunt, sive acatholici ad eam *conversi,* conversione quidem non ex privato agendi modo corrivata, sed ex actu iuxta Ecclesiae ritum peracto, qui adscriptionem in catholicorum coetum secumfert. An vero his infantes sint accensendi, qui licet acatholice baptizati, a parentibus *conversis,* vel aliis horum legitimo loco, catholice dein educantur, haud indubia res est, licet Auctores non desint qui in affirmativam sententiam inclinare videantur. Et dubium non immerito ipse Codex ingerit . . ."—*S. Romanae Rotae Decisiones seu Sententiae* (Romae, 1912—), XVIII (1926), 314.

before this line of reasoning can be followed. If the validity of the baptism after due investigation remains doubtful, the person must be baptized *sub conditione*. However, if the child attended a Catholic school for a few years but received most of its training in public schools, or if the child has no idea of the Catholic doctrine, or if the child was brought to church to attend Mass only once in a long while, then one cannot say that the child is a convert. The practice of the Catholic Faith must be constant. It must be noted that a *conversio interna* does not effect a change in the person's relationship to one particular religion; a *conversio externa* is necessary.[23]

According to the teaching of the Church there is never a just cause for a person's apostasy if he once knowingly and willingly professed the Faith.[24] It is because of this that the Church in canon 1099, § 1, prescribes that apostasy does not exempt an apostate from the obligation to observe the juridical form of marriage, whether the apostatized person was a Catholic from birth or was converted to the Catholic Faith in later life. Relative to the continued subjection to the law of the Church on the juridical form for the contraction of marriage it is inconsequently whether the Catholic Faith has been rejected entirely or only partially. It is immaterial whether those who have defected from the Faith have lapsed into irreligion and unbelief, or whether they have become associates in a non-Catholic religion. The term *deficere* has a purely negative connotation.

Catholics are bound to observe the form for the celebration of matrimony even if they contract a marriage with non-Catholics.[25] As regards the form, it is unimportant whether the non-Catholics with whom the Catholics enter into a marriage are baptized or not. The obligation of the Catholic party to observe the form of marriage is not changed by the fact that he marries a non-Catholic who is not baptized. In other words, not only parties of whom both are Catholics, but also parties of whom one is a non-Catholic must observe the juridical form of marriage. Mixed marriages must be understood

[23] Triebs, *op. cit.*, p. 607.

[24] Cf. Hervé, *Manuale Theologiae Dogmaticae,* III, 341.

[25] Can. 1099, § 1, n. 2: "Iidem, de quibus supra, si cum acatholicis sive baptizatis sive non baptizatis etiam post obtentam dispensationem ab impedimento mixtae religionis vel disparitatis cultus matrimonium contrahant."

in the sense of marriages on the part of Catholics with baptized non-Catholics as well as of Catholics with infidels.[26]

According to the present legislation a person who is bound to observe the form of marriage when marrying a person who is not bound by this obligation transmits the obligation of observing the form to the person not otherwise bound by it. This follows the principle: "*Pars ligata communicat alteria suum ligamen.* In earlier legislation, i. e., under the decree "*Tametsi,*" the person who was free of the obligation communicated his freedom to the person who was bound by the obligation. But in the present law, if a Catholic who is bound to observe the form for the celebration of marriage marries a non-Catholic who is exempt by positive legislation from this obligation, then the non-Catholic is bound to observe the form in this particular case because of the obligation that the Catholic has. Formerly, under the decree "*Tametsi,*" however, the Catholic was not bound by this obligation provided that the non-Catholic was not bound by it.[27]

Catholics of the various Oriental rites are not bound by the ecclesiastical laws of the Code, unless it be expressly mentioned in the Code that the law pertains to the members of the Oriental rite also.[28] The legislation on the juridical form of marriage does not embrace the subjects of the Oriental Church, for they are not expressly included under it. Hence the Orientals are not bound to observe the form of marriage in virtue of the law of the Code, when they contract a marriage among themselves or with heretics or schismatics. But if they contract a marriage with a Catholic of the Latin rite, they are bound to observe the form in view of the standing principle: *Pars ligata communicat alteri suum ligamen.*[29]

This legislation was taken over from pre-Code law. The S.

[26] Canon 1099, § 1, expressly mentions that the dispensation from mixed religion or disparity of worship does not include a dispensation from the juridical form of marriage.

[27] Gasparri, *De Matrimonio,* n. 1021.

[28] Can. 1. Cf. Gasparri, *op. cit.,* n. 1022.

[29] This is also expressed in canon 1099, § 1, n. 3. Cf. Ayrinhac, *Marriage Legislation,* p. 268. He states: "Catholics of the various Oriental rites, e. g., Maronites, Copts, etc. (eight rites), are affected by the law when they marry Latins who are subject to the Catholic form of marriage."

Congregation of the Council decided on February 1, 1908, that Catholics of the Oriental rite were not bound to observe the prescriptions of the decree *"Ne temere"* when they contracted marriage among themselves.[80] On March 28, 1908, the same S. Congregation decided that a Catholic of the Latin rite when marrying a Catholic of the Oriental rite was bound to observe the form of marriage enacted in the decree *"Ne temere."* [81]

Inasmuch as the decree *"Tametsi"* of the Council of Trent had been promulgated among the Ruthenians of Galicia and Syria, the S. Congregation for the Propagation of the Faith ruled that these members of the Oriental rite were bound to observe the prescriptions of the decree *"Ne temere,"* and hence were bound to observe the form of marriage just as the Catholics of the Latin rite.[82] This legislation was extended by the Sacred Congregation for the Propagation of the Faith to the Ruthenians of the United States of North America on August 17, 1914.[83] The decree *"Cum data fuerit"* issued on March 1, 1929, by the S. Congregation for the Oriental Church repeated the former legislation as regards the form of marriage. The decree states that marriages, both between Greek-Ruthenians and between the faithful of different rites, must be contracted with the observance of the form prescribed by the decree *Ne temere;* and hence they are to be blessed in the rite of the woman, by the woman's pastor.[84] In 1940, the same Sacred Congregation added that if there

[80] S. C. C., 1 febr. 1908: "I.—An decreto *Ne temere* astringantur etiam catholici ritus Orientalis. . . ." "'Ad I—*Negative.*"

[81] S. C. C., 28 mart. 1908: "I.—Utrum validum sit matrimonium contractum a catholico ritus latini cum catholico ritus orientalis non servata forma a decreto 'Ne temere' statuta." "Ad I—*Negative.*"

[82] S. C. Prop. Fidei, 5 maii 1911: "Nihilo minus caput *Tametsi* est promulgatum inter Ruthenos Galliciae et fortasse etiam in Syria. Ruthenos autem Gallicianae provinciae (non autem alios), *S. C. de Propaganda Fide* pro negotiis ritus Orientalis, decreto 5 maii 1911, legi *Ne temere* obnoxios fecit."—*Periodica,* XIV (1925), 102-103.

[83] S. C. de Prop. Fide, decr., 17 aug. 1914, Art. 30: "Matrimonia tum inter fideles Graeco-Ruthenos, tum inter fideles mixti ritus, servata forma decreti *Ne temere,* contrahi debent, ac proinde in ritu mulieris a parocho mulieris benedicenda sunt."—*AAS,* VI (1914), 463.

[84] S. C. pro Eccl. Orient., decr., *"Cum data fuerit,"* 1 mart. 1929, Art. 39: "Matrimonia tum inter fideles Graeco-Ruthenos tum inter fideles mixti ritus,

is a just reason therefor, such marriages may be celebrated in the rite of the man, according to the judgment and with the consent of the ordinary of the place.[85] Cappello, it must be noted, is very definite in his statement that the decree *Ne temere* constitutes the law for the Ruthenians in this country.[86]

2. Who is Exempt From the Form?

Non-Catholics, whether baptized or unbaptized, are not bound to observe the juridical form of marriage when they contract marriages among themselves.[87] As regards the unbaptized, this legislation can be understood very easily, for such persons cannot be bound by any law of purely ecclesiastical origin, inasmuch as they are not members of the Church of Christ.[88] But as regards the baptized, while they are ordinarily bound by the laws of purely ecclesiastical origin, canon 1099, § 2, expressly exempts them by positive legislation from the obligation to observe the form of marriage. In other words, it is the express intention of the legislator not to include baptized non-Catholics under this law. While it is true that the Church does not profess the same direct interest in the marriages between baptized non-Catholics as it professes in the marriages between Catholics, yet the Church of necessity has an interest in the marriages between baptized non-Catholics when there is question of the dissolution of such marriages which paves the way for one of the parties to contract a new marriage with a Catholic.[89]

The validity of marriages between unbaptized non-Catholics depends on the laws of the country where the marriage is contracted. For unbaptized persons marrying among themselves civil authority may decree diriment impediments and invalidating laws. The State

servata forma decreti 'Ne temere' contrahi debent, ac proinde in ritu mulieris a parocho mulieris benedicenda sunt."—*AAS,* XXI (1929), 152.

[85] S. C. pro Eccl. Orient., 23 nov. 1940, Art. 39: "Quod si iusta causa adsit, proterunt nuptiae celebrari in ritu viri, de iudicio et consensu Ordinarii loci."—*AAS,* XXXIII (1941), 27; cf. *The Jurist,* I (1941), 267.

[86] Cappello, *De Matrimonio,* III, nn. 924-925.

[87] Can. 1099, § 2.

[88] Cf. can. 12.

[89] Triebs, *Handbuch des kanonischen Eherechts,* p. 609.

can also prescribe the observance of a specified form for the marriages of unbaptized persons. But the State cannot set up the requirement of a specific form for the valid contraction of marriages between baptized non-Catholics, or between baptized and unbaptized non-Catholics. The Church has the exclusive right to legislate concerning marriages of baptized persons. The Church has expressly exempted baptized non-Catholics from the observance of the juridical form of marriage. But as far as the impediments are concerned, as long as the Church does not expressly exempt Christians from the laws of purely ecclesiastical origin, they are bound by the impediments. The impediment of consanguinity, for example, binds all baptized persons, whether they are members of the Catholic Church or members of a heretical sect. The impediment of disparity of worship, on the other hand, binds only Catholics, because the Church again expressly exempts baptized non-Catholics when they contract a marriage with an infidel.[40] As a matter of fact, baptized non-Catholics are exempt from only two of the Church's laws which deal with hindrances that militate against the valid contraction of marriage by a baptized Christian. These two laws deal with the impediment of disparity of cult and the required observance of a specific juridical form for the contraction of marriage. Baptized non-Catholics are subjects to all the other laws of the Church in relation to the valid contraction of marriage.

Canon 1099, § 2, introduces new legislation according to which Titus, who is born of non-Catholic parents, but baptized in the Catholic Church, is considered as a non-Catholic with regard to the legislation on the form of marriage, provided that he was reared from infancy in heresy, schism, Judaism, Islamism, atheism, or infidelity and provided that he contracts marriage with a non-Catholic.[41] Therefore the following suppositions may be made to clarify this new provision:

a. If Titus, born of parents one of whom was not a Catholic, baptized in the Catholic Church, but reared from infancy outside the Faith, wishes to marry a Catholic, he must observe the form be-

[40] Can. 1070, § 1. Cf. Alford, "Common Law Marriage in Relation to the Code,"—*The Jurist,* II (1942), 248-262.

[41] Cf. *infra,* pp. 63, 64.

cause of the principle: *Pars ligata communicat alteri suum ligamen.* The Catholic is subject to the form, and hence Titus is bound also.

b. If Titus, born of parents one of whom was not a Catholic, baptized in the Catholic Church, was reared in the Catholic Faith, he himself is bound to observe the form.

c. If Titus was born of Catholic parents who were practical Catholics, was baptized in the Catholic Church, but reared in heresy, schism, or infidelity, he is also bound to observe the form. Such a case can easily obtain if the Catholic parents, for example, died soon after the baptism of the child, and the child was given to the custody of non-Catholic relatives; or, again, if the parents defected from the Faith soon after the baptism of the child, and then reared the child in heresy, schism or infidelity.[42]

According to Triebs,[43] if Titus was born of Catholic parents, baptized in the Catholic Church, but reared in heresy, schism or infidelity, he is not bound by the form of marriage, because he never willingly and knowingly belonged to the Catholic Church. But this doctrine seems to be contrary to the legislation of the Code. The Code expressly states that only the children who are born of non-Catholic parents are exempt from the observance of the juridical form. Therefore, if both parents are practical Catholics, or even indifferent Catholics, at the time of the birth of the child, and if they have the child baptized in the Catholic Church, but rear it in heresy, schism or infidelity, the child is subject to the form of marriage.

All baptized people are subject to the Church's laws on marriage unless they are expressly exempted. Now, such an exemption is not made in canon 1099 for a person baptized in the Catholic Church as the offspring of Catholic parents. A baptized person becomes subject through infant baptism to a long list of obligations for the assumption and recognition of which he has not declared himself with any conscious or positive act of the will.

That a child born of Catholic parents, baptized in the Catholic Church, but reared in heresy, schism or infidelity, is bound to observe the form of marriage is also the opinion of Cappello.[44]

[42] Jone, *Gesetzbuch des kanonischen Rechtes,* II, 321.

[43] *Handbuch des kanonischen Eherechts,* p. 610.

[44] *De Matrimonio,* III, n. 702 ad 5, which states: "Nati a parentibus

d. If Titus was born of parents one of whom was a non-Catholic, was baptized in the Catholic Church but reared in heresy, schism or infidelity from infancy, he is not subject to the form when he contracts marriage with a non-Catholic. But suppose he wishes to marry Bertha who is in the same situation as himself. For Bertha was also born of non-Catholic parents, was baptized in the Catholic Church but reared in heresy, schism or infidelity from infancy. Bertha, of course, is not bound to observe the form when she contracts marriage with a non-Catholic. But the case is such that Titus wishes to marry Bertha. The question arises, are they bound to observe the form? The solution to this question hinges on the interpretation of the words *cum parte acatholica* of canon 1099, § 2. The term *non-Catholic* with whom these persons can contract a marriage seems to embrace not only those who were not baptized in the Catholic Church, but also those who were born of non-Catholic parents, were baptized in the Catholic Church, but then reared from infancy in heresy, schism or infidelity.[45] Therefore Titus and Bertha are not bound to observe the form of marriage when they contract a marriage between each other.

e. Children born of apostatized parents, provided the parents apostatized before the birth of the child,[46] must be considered under the rule here indicated. In other words, a person who was born of parents who had apostatized before his birth and who was baptized in the Catholic Church, but reared from infancy in heresy, schism or

catholicis, baptizati in Ecclesia catholica, qui ab infantili aetate adoleverint extra religionem catholicam, tenentur servare statutam formam canonicam celebrationis matrimonii."

[45] Jone, *Gesetzbuch des kanonischen Rechtes,* II, 321; Gasparri (*op. cit.,* n. 1023) states: "*Etsi in Ecclesia catholica baptizati,* quia baptizati extra Ecclesiam catholicam sunt acatholici qui comprehenduntur in prima parte part. 2." This implies that these persons are non-Catholics who are baptized in the Catholic Church, for the first part of paragraph 2 treats of non-Catholics who are baptized outside the Catholic Church. Cf. also Noldin-Schmitt, *Summa Theologiae Moralis,* III, 653, n. 644. Wernz-Vidal (*Ius Matrimoniale,* n. 552) state: "Acatholicis accensentur, in ordine ad hanc legem, 'ab acatholicis nati, etsi in Ecclesia catholica baptizati, qui ab infantili aetate in haeresi vel schismate aut infidelitate vel sine ulla religione adoleverunt.' "

[46] *Cf. supra,* p. 64.

infidelity, would not be subject to the juridical form of marriage, if such a person contracted a marriage with a non-Catholic.

f. A person who was born of Catholic parents, but was baptized outside the Catholic Church, is not bound to observe the form, if he was reared in heresy, schism or infidelity from infancy; but such a person is bound to observe the form, if he was reared in the Catholic Faith.[47]

It must be noted that, while such persons are exempt from the observance of the form of marriage, they are subject to all the impediments of ecclesiastical law, especially the impediment of disparity of worship. Hence, it may happen that a marriage is invalid because the parties have failed to petition the competent authority for a dispensation from the impediment which existed between them, although they were exempt from the requirement of the juridical form of marriage. However, the question is not as simple as it at first appears. If someone was born of non-Catholic parents or of a mixed marriage, was baptized in the Catholic Church, but reared in heresy, schism or infidelity, he is considered as a non-Catholic in his exemption from the obligation of observing the form of marriage. From this it could seem to follow that, if he wishes to marry an infidel, he is not bound by the impediment of disparity of worship, for in relation to the law on the form of marriage he is considered to be a non-Catholic. On the other hand, by the Church's own positive enactment the diriment impediment of disparity of worship does not bind baptized non-Catholics in their marriages with infidels.[48] However, the Holy Office in a single case has decided the contrary.[49] The question was by no means solved by this decision, for the decision was never promulgated, and it concerned one case which involved many particular circumstances.[50] But on August 29, 1940, the Pontifical Commission replied in the affirmative to the following question: "Whether persons born of non-Catholics, mentioned in canon

[47] Cappello, *op. cit.*, n. 702.

[48] Can. 1070, § 1: "Nullum est matrimonium contractum a persona non baptizata cum persona baptizata in Ecclesia catholica vel ad eandem ex haeresi aut schismate conversa."

[49] S. C. S. Off., 1 maii 1922—*AKKR,* XVII (1922), 180.

[50] Cf. *Periodica,* XX (1931), 75.

1099, § 2, are bound, according to canon 1070, by the impediment of disparity of worship when they contract marriage with an unbaptized person." [51]

By reason of this decision one must conclude that a person who was born of non-Catholic parents, was baptized in the Catholic Church, but was reared from infancy in heresy, schism or infidelity, needs a dispensation from the impediment of disparity of worship when he contracts a marriage with an infidel, but can contract the marriage without being subject to the law on the form. Of course, it is quite possible for a marriage to be invalid because of the presence of some diriment impediment even though its contraction was not invalidated by any lack of compliance with a juridically required form. The Protestant Titus, for example, marries his Protestant cousin Bertha without obtaining a dispensation from the diriment impediment of consanguinity. The marriage is contracted before either a Protestant minister or a civil judge. This marriage is actually invalid by reason of the impediment of consanguinity, but there is no absence of validity in relation to the form in which it was contracted, for these persons were not subject to the requirement of the form inasmuch as canon 1099, § 2, has expressly exempted them.

It is to be noted that, if the Protestant father reared the child officially as a non-Catholic, even though the child had been baptized in the Catholic Church, but the Catholic mother instructed the child privately in the Catholic Faith, then, according to the interpretation of canon 1099, § 2, one cannot speak of a non-Catholic education as received by this child. Therefore such a child when grown would be bound to observe the form of marriage. In the same manner, if a child was born of Catholic parents, was baptized in a heretical sect, but was reared from infancy in the Catholic Faith, such a child when grown would be subject to the form of marriage, even in the event that there was a contraction of marriage with a non-Catholic party.[52]

What is meant by the expression *ab infantili aetate?* This phrase

[51] *AAS,* XXXII (1940), 212. Cf. Bouscaren, *1941 Supplement,* p. 128, under can. 1070.

[52] Triebs, *op. cit.,* p. 610.

implies that one has to go back to a time before the child reached the use of reason, and that after the child has reached the use of reason the parents continue to rear it in a heretical, schismatical or pagan sect. The child thus remains a non-Catholic, though it has been baptized in the Catholic Church. Such a child when grown would not be held to the form of marriage, for after such a person has completed his formal education, he follows the non-Catholic religion not by reason of a positive act of the will to remain a non-Catholic, but merely by reason of a habitual status. Therefore, he does not willingly and knowingly reject the Catholic Faith, but remains a non-Catholic purely because of his non-Catholic training. The fact that the person remembers a few Catholic prayers is not an indication that he has received a Catholic education.[53] In these cases the Church shows a rather favorable consideration to the party concerned. The reason for this lies in the fact that the Church does not wish to impose obligations on a person when the person is innocent. This case must not be confused with the case of those who knowingly and willingly belonged to the Church, but later apostatized or defected from it.

Only an investigation into the circumstances of the case can determine whether or not a person is reared from infancy in heresy, schism or infidelity. If the person has received first Holy Communion or has attended a Catholic school for a number of years, the exemptions granted in canon 1099, § 2, do not obtain, and hence the party would be bound to observe the form, even though he was reared in heresy, schism or infidelity for a number of years. The fact that a child has been educated in heresy, schism or infidelity for a number of years does not restrict the interpretation of the phrase *ab infantili aetate,* or excuse him from the observance of the law. The phrase *ab infantili aetate* means exactly what the words imply, namely, from infancy; it does not mean from the eighth, ninth or tenth year of the child's life. It is true that the child may have fallen away from the Catholic Faith through no fault of its own, but that would not justify any interpretation of the phrase in such a wide sense that anyone who apostatized before contracting a mar-

[53] Cf. *infra,* Chap. VI, p. 142.

riage, no matter at what age, would escape the legislation on the juridical form required for the valid celebration of marriage, and could thus rightly consider himself to share in the exemption of canon 1099, § 2. Such an interpretation surely runs counter to the law and the intention of the legislator.

The meaning of the words *"ab acatholicis nati"* of canon 1099, § 2, was once greatly controverted. Most of the authors understood the words as relating to only such marriages in which both of the parties were non-Catholics. This opinion, however, had to be discarded when the Pontifical Commission issued its answer on the question.[54] This reply stated that the prescriptions of canon 1099, § 2, were verified when the child was born of a mixed marriage, that is, of a marriage in which one party was a Catholic and the other party a non-Catholic, irrespective of the fact whether or not the parties signed the prenuptial promises as required by law.[55]

This answer appears to be based on the justified assumption that to a certain extent the children of mixed marriages are no more favored in their Faith than are the children of completely non-Catholic marriages. In many cases the Catholic party is indeed able to enforce the baptism of the child in the Catholic Church, but is not able to exert any positive influence on the education of the child. It may also happen that the Catholic party dies before the child can receive any education, so that the child's education is left to the non-Catholic spouse.[56]

To the question whether its authentic interpretation was solely declarative or also extensive in its character, the Pontifical Commission answered: *"Affirmative ad primam partem."* [57] This means that the legislator always understood the phrase *"ab acatholicis nati"* as embracing the children born to marriages of Catholics with non-

[54] Pont. Comm. Intr., 20 iul. 1929: "D.—An *ab acatholicis nati,* de quibus in canone 1099, § 2, dicendi sint etiam nati ab alterutro parente acatholico, cautionibus quoque praestitis ad normam canonum 1061 et 1071. R.—Affirmative."—*AAS,* XX (1929), 573.

[55] Cf. cans. 1061 and 1071.

[56] Triebs, *op. cit.,* p. 611.

[57] Pont. Comm. Intr., 25 iul. 1931: "D.—Utrum interpretatio diei 20 iulii 1929 ad canonem 1099, § 2, sit declarativa, an extensiva. R.—Affirmative ad primam partem, negative ad secundam."—*AAS,* XXIII (1931), 388.

Catholics as well as those born to the marriages between non-Catholics. Therefore, the interpretation had to be regarded as being retroactive in its juridical force and efficacy.[58] This was explained by the Holy Office in a concrete case.[59] However, in the same year the Holy Office reserved to itself the right to decide on the validity of such marriages which had been contracted before the publication of the decision by the Pontifical Commission. This reservation was never made public; but from it one is inclined to infer that the Holy Office considered the answer of the Pontifical Commission to be explanatory rather than merely declarative in character.[60]

On February 17, 1930, the Pontifical Commission declared that the words *"ab acatholicis nati"* of canon 1099, § 2, had to be understood as including also the children of apostates.[61] Apostates are those who have completely rejected the Christian Faith. The case would be verified if, for example, erstwhile Catholics professed the teachings of Judaism or Islamism.[62] But also those who have rejected the Catholic Faith without professing any particular non-Christian teaching are apostates. According to the interpretation of the Pontifical Commission the children of apostates, whether both parents apostatized or only one, are not bound to observe the form. It is understood, however, that the parents apostatized before the child was born, otherwise the child is born of Catholic parents, and hence the exemption cannot be applied.[63] If the child was born of Catholic parents who shortly after the baptism of the child apostatized, and then reared the child in infidelity, the child when grown would be bound to observe the form as has been explained previously.

[58] Can. 17, § 2: "Interpretatio authentica, per modum legis exhibita, eandem vim habet ac lex ipsa; et si verba legis in se certa declaret tantum, promulgatione non eget et valet retrorsum. . . ."

[59] S. C. S. Off., 9 iun. 1931—*Periodica,* XXI (1932), 14.

[60] *Periodica,* XXI (1932), 46.

[61] Pont. Comm. Intr., 17 febr. 1930: "D.—An sub verbis: *ab acatholicis nati,* de quibus in canone 1099, § 2, comprehendantur etiam nati ab apostatis. R.—Affirmative."—*AAS,* XXII (1930), 195.

[62] Can. 1325, § 2: "Post receptum baptismum si quis, nomen retinens christianum, pertinaciter aliquam ex veritatibus fide divina et catholica credendis denegat aut de ea dubitat, haereticus; si a fide christiana totaliter recedit, apostata; . . ."

[63] Cf. *supra,* pp. 57, 58.

In relation to the cases of apostates one must be particularly careful not to confuse apostasy with indifferentism. There are many indifferent Catholics, who cannot be considered apostates in the sense of the law. Children of indifferent Catholics are not included in the exemption granted by canon 1099, § 2.

The exemption from the law on the requisite form is a very liberal one. The reason is to be sought perhaps in the fact that the Church wishes to preclude the possibility of a large number of null and void marriages consequent to the defect in the form of their contraction. This idea was also prevalent at the time of the Council of Trent, when the Church ordered a singular method for the promulgation of the law "*Tametsi.*" In order to avoid the multiplication of invalid marriages by heretics who would not observe this new juridical form for the celebration of marriage, the Council of Trent decreed that the *Tametsi* law was to be published in each individual parish at the discretion of the bishop and it was to take effect thirty days from the date of promulgation.[64] Thus, where it was seen that the majority of the inhabitants in a particular diocese were Catholic, the *Tametsi* decree was promulgated in the individual parishes. Where this condition did not exist, the decree was not published.

[64] Concilium Tridentinum, sess. XXIV, *de ref. matrim,* c. 1.

CHAPTER V

THE COMPETENT AUTHORITY FOR THE DECLARATION OF NULLITY

ACCORDING to the *Instruction* of 1936 the cases of the declaration of nullity of a marriage contracted outside the Church *"solvendi sunt ab Ordinario ipso, vel a parocho, consulto Ordinario . . ."* From this it is evident that the number of persons who are competent to grant a declaration of nullity is rather extensive.

The competency of the ordinary or pastor is determined by the domicile or quasi-domicile of either party.

The Code, when ruling on the acquisition of a domicile or quasi-domicile, simply states that a domicile is acquired by residence in any parish or quasi-parish, or at least in a diocese, vicariate apostolic or prefecture apostolic, if it has lasted for ten years or is combined with the intention of remaining in the place permanently. A quasi-domicile is acquired by residence in a parish, or a diocese, if it has lasted for the greater part of a year or is combined with the intention of staying there for the greater part of the year, unless something calls one away.[1]

Domicile, in general, means one's fixed residence. The Code itself does not state that only those who are baptized can acquire a domicile or quasi-domicile, but it seems rather to include anyone who has taken up residence in a particular territory, whether it be in a parish or in a diocese. Hence, as far as the domicile or quasi-domicile is concerned, it is immaterial of itself what religion is professed by the person who has taken up residence. An infidel can establish a domicile as well as a baptized person, provided that the infidel resides within the territorial limits of a parish or a diocese, and provided that all the other elements of the law are fulfilled. The Church, while not making a law for the unbaptized, merely recognizes a juridical fact which can attach to the lives of the unbaptized as well as to the lives of the baptized.[2]

[1] Can. 92.

[2] *AAS,* VIII (1916), 65.

Ordinarily and directly the ordinary or the pastor cannot exercise jurisdiction over those who are not their subjects. The ordinary or the pastor can exercise jurisdiction only over those who are baptized, and hence all unbaptized persons are excluded from the jurisdiction of the ordinary or the pastor. Indirectly, however, the ordinary or the pastor may exercise jurisdiction over the infidel. Such a condition obtains, for example, when the infidel attempts to contract a marriage with a Catholic either civilly or in the presence of a non-Catholic minister and later desires to marry another Catholic. Then the ordinary or pastor may exercise his jurisdictional power indirectly over this person.

For the celebration of marriage, parochial domicile is the consideration of primary importance; in the matter of competency in matrimonial cases, diocesan domicile is the important factor. The person competent to grant a decree of nullity is the ordinary or pastor of the place in which either party has a domicile or quasi-domicile; or, in the case of a Catholic and a non-Catholic, the ordinary or the pastor of the place in which the Catholic has a domicile or a quasi-domicile.

Canon 91 says that a *vagus* is one who has neither a domicile nor a quasi-domicile. Canon 94, § 2, further states that the proper pastor or ordinary of a *vagus* is the pastor or ordinary of the place where the *vagus* is actually residing at the time. Therefore, the ordinary or the pastor of the place where the *vagus* is actually residing may grant a decree of nullity to the *vagus*.

1. The Ordinary

The meaning of the term ordinary can be gathered from the Code of Canon Law.[8] The term embraces a number of persons, and is not restricted to the person of the residential bishop of the diocese. In law the name *ordinary* includes, aside from the Roman Pontiff, all residential bishops. They are the ordinaries for the territory entrusted to their care. It also includes the abbot or prelate *nullius*, the vicar general of the residential bishop as well as of the abbot or prelate *nullius*, the apostolic administrator, the vicar and prefect apostolic. Furthermore, those persons are ordinaries who succeed to

[8] Can. 198.

the office during vacancy either by the provisions of law or in virtue of approved constitutions, such as the diocesan administrator who is elected by the diocesan consultors upon the death of the bishop.[4] In exempt clerical religious institutes, the major superior is the ordinary over his subjects.

The government of the diocese must be entrusted to the care of a bishop.[5] Since the episcopal office is of divine institution, it can never be abrogated. As successors of the Apostoles residential bishops have the ordinary powers of office which accrued to the office of the Apostles. They have the power to govern the people who come under their jurisdiction. Residential bishops do not enjoy the personal extraordinary powers of the Apostles, such as the power to perform miracles, the power of personal infallibility, etc. But the power by which bishops govern their dioceses is ordinary power, dependent on the Roman Pontiff.

The declaration of the nullity of a marriage normally entails an administrative process, and hence falls under the exercise of voluntary jurisdiction. The bishop has that jurisdiction by divine institution, and therefore he is competent to declare a marriage null when the parties have failed to comply with the form required by the law of the Church.

The major superiors included in the name *ordinary* are the major superiors of exempt clerical institutes. Only in such institutes do the major superiors enjoy the power of jurisdiction over their subjects. The superiors of non-exempt clerical institutes or of lay institutes have only dominative power over their subjects. But the question arises whether the major superior of an exempt clerical institute is included under the term *ordinary* in Article 231 of the Instruction. It is true that the Instruction simply mentions the *Ordinarius* and not the *Ordinarius loci.* If the Instruction would state that the *Ordinarius loci* may settle these cases, it would be plain that the major superiors would not be included.[6]

[4] Cf. can. 432.

[5] Can. 329, § 1: "Episcopi sunt Apostolorum successores atque ex divina institutione peculiaribus ecclesiis praeficiuntur quas cum potestate ordinaria regunt sub auctoritate Romani Pontificis."

[6] Can. 198, § 2: "Nomine autem *Ordinarii loci* seu *locorum* veniunt omnes recensiti, exceptis Superioribus religiosis."

Now, it is clear that the article refers to pastors upon whom it is incumbent to make the necessary investigations concerning the free status of the parties according to the norms of canon 1019, and who are then competent to render a declaration of nullity of marriages contracted outside the Church. But it is quite evident that the *pastor* there mentioned is the *parochus loci* who has a right to assist at the marriage. It is the pastor of the place where the parties have a domicile or quasi-domicile. It can be argued from this that the ordinary must be the ordinary of the place where the parties have a domicile or quasi-domicile and thereby are constituted his subjects. The article, then, seems to refer to the local ordinary.

There are some canons in the Code which simply mention the *Ordinarius,* but in which it appears that the major superior of an exempt clerical institute is not included. Thus, for example, in canon 1990 the Code simply mentions the *Ordinarius,* but the major superior is not there included under the term.[7] Therefore, the major religious superior of exempt clerical institutes must be held not competent to grant a decree of nullity.[8]

In every diocese there should be an official, who is a priest designated by the bishop to act as judge. He has ordinary power to judge all cases that the bishop has not reserved to himself. The official exercises the judicial power of the bishop. He does not take care of matters of administrative procedure. But since the declaration of nullity is a purely administrative procedure, the official is not competent to decide these cases by reason of his office. However, he may be delegated to take care of these cases and thus will obtain the necessary competency. But inasmuch as the official is preoccupied with the judicial cases that come to the attention of the diocesan tribunal, it would be much better if the vicar general were to take care of all cases of nullity. This would expedite the matter and would remove a burden from the official. Since the vicar general is competent by reason of his office, why should someone else be delegated? If in a diocese the offices of vicar general and of official are

[7] Keene, *Religious Ordinaries and Canon 198,* The Catholic University of America Canon Law Studies, n. 135 (Washington, D. C.: The Catholic University of America Press, 1942), p. 13.

[8] Cf. cans. 198; 615; 488, n. 4.

vested in the same person, then this person would be competent to grant decrees of nullity, not by reason of his office of official, but by reason of his office of vicar general.[9]

It is the obligation of the bishop to appoint in the diocesan curia a chancellor whose duty it is to keep the files of the diocesan curia and the archives of the diocese in good order. The chancellor does not have the power of jurisdiction, but certain powers may be delegated to him by the bishop. If the bishop gives him the faculty to issue decrees of nullity, the chancellor is certainly competent. But why should the bishop delegate the chancellor for certain administrative and jurisdictional acts, when these things can easily be taken care of by the vicar general, who does not need delegation, but acts by reason of his office?

To declare a marriage null is an exercise of voluntary jurisdiction, which is not enjoyed by the chancellor as such. The practice of habitually employing the priest who is the chancellor for the continual and universal exercise of delegated jurisdiction is contrary to the spirit of the Code. This has been explained thoroughly by Prince.[10] However, the chancellor may be delegated in particular cases, for example, in the absence of the vicar general; or he may be delegated for a short period of time, such as three or four weeks. This seems to be more in accord with the spirit of the Code.[11]

2. The Pastor

The pastor is an individual priest or a moral person, such as a college, a chapter, etc., to whom a parish has been given *in titulum*.[12]

[9] Cf. can. 1573.

[10] *The Diocesan Chancellor,* The Catholic University of America Canon Law Studies, n. 167 (Washington, D. C.: The Catholic University of America Press, 1942), pp. 90-101.

[11] Jone, *Gesetzbuch des kanonischen Rechtes,* I, 204.

[12] Woywod (*A Practical Commentary on the Code of Canon Law* [5. ed., 2 vols., New York: Joseph F. Wagner, 1939], I, 160) translates the phrase *in titulum* "with rightful possession," designating the office, rights and duties of the legal holder of the parish. Jone (*op. cit.*, I, 352) explains that the Latin expression *in titulum* indicates that the parish carries the marks of him who receives it. Hence the parish belongs to him and he can carry out all acts of his office by reason of ordinary power and not merely with delegated jurisdiction.

Beginning with the time that the pastor takes possession of his parish, he has the right and the office to care for the temporal and spiritual welfare of his parishioners. The parishioners are those who have a domicile or quasi-domicile within the territorial limits in which the pastor is entrusted with pastoral authority. According to the Instruction of 1936 the pastor is competent to declare a marriage null, if the parties neglected to observe the required form. But before he can proceed to grant a declaration of nullity, he must have consulted the ordinary. This consultation with the ordinary, however, does not pertain to the validity of the act. If a pastor grants a decree of nullity after having made the necessary investigations into the case, but without having consulted the ordinary previously, the decree of nullity is valid, but the pastor acts illicitly. The pastor has that right by reason of his office. This right may be limited and restricted. But it cannot be restricted to such an extent as to take it away completely, for by doing that one would destroy the office itself. Therefore, the act of the pastor is always valid, but it is not always licit.

Under the name of *pastor* must be included the quasi-pastor,[13] the acting vicar,[14] the parochial administrator,[15] the parochial substitute,[16] and the parochial adjutant.[17] As regards the parochial adjutant, he must be appointed by the bishop if a pastor is no longer able to care for his parish because of sickness, mental or physical. This appointment can be made even though the pastor is unwilling to accept one. If the parochial adjutant takes the pastor's place in all things, he has the same rights and obligations as the pastor with the exception of the duty of applying the *Missa pro populo*. The parochial adjutant has ordinary jurisdiction, and hence he is competent to grant a decree of nullity. If, however, the pastor is only partially disabled, then the powers of the parochial adjutant must be determined from the letter of appointment. Since in the latter case the parochial adjutant does not have all the rights of a pastor,

[13] Cf. cans. 451, § 2; 216, § 3.

[14] Cf. can. 471.

[15] Cf. can. 472.

[16] Cf. can. 474.

[17] Cf. can. 475.

he cannot be included under the term of pastor. Therefore, under these peculiar circumstances he is not competent *per se* to act in cases of the nullity of marriages, unless this power has been granted to him in his letter of appointment, or unless the pastor has delegated him to take care of the cases of evident nullity.

If the pastor cannot take care of his parish because of the large number of the faithful or the extensive territory of his parish, the ordinary is to appoint a parochial assistant to help the pastor. This parochial assistant is commonly known as a curate in certain parts of this country. The rights and obligations of the assistant must be determined from the diocesan statutes, from the episcopal letter of appointment and from the commission which the pastor gives to the assistant. But if nothing has been expressly provided in any of the aforesaid ways, then the assistant has the obligation to help the pastor in all things that pertain to the parochial office. The only exception is that the assistant does not have the obligation to say the *Missa pro populo* for the pastor.[18]

In connection with the status of a parochial assistant there arose a great controversy among authors, namely, whether the assistant has ordinary or delegated jurisdiction. Some authors [19] are of the opinion that the assistants have ordinary jurisdiction by reason of their office, which is of such an extent as is provided for in the diocesan statutes, in the letter of appointment or by the pastor himself. However, the chief objection to this theory is that according to canon 451, § 2, n. 2, the assistants are not included in the term of pastor. If they were, then the norms of canon 462 concerning the functions reserved to the pastor, and the norms of canon 463 concerning the right of the pastor to the stole-fees, would be superflous.

Eichmann [20] claims that in the absence of the pastor the assistant has ordinary jurisdiction to the same extent as the pastor, unless the pastor has restricted it, whereas when the pastor is present, the assistant has delegated jurisdiction. The criticism of this explana-

[18] Cf. can. 476.

[19] Coronata, *Institutiones Iuris Canonici,* I, 597; Haring, "Die Jurisdiktion des Pfarrvikars,"—*Theol.-prakt. Quartalschrift,* LXXV (1922), 24; Augustine, *A Commentary on the New Code of Canon Law* (8 vols., Vol. II, 6. ed., St. Louis: Herder Book Co., 1936), II, 575-576.

[20] *Lehrbuch,* I, 259.

tion is that if one considers the norms of canon 476, § 6, alone, one may translate it to mean that the assistant by reason of his office has an obligation to substitute for the pastor. But that explanation does not fit in with paragraph 1 of the same canon which states that the assistant is an aid to and not a substitute of the pastor. Furthermore, a substitute is always appointed during the absence of the pastor.[21]

Hilling [22] defends the opinion that the assistant has partly ordinary and partly delegated jurisdiction. As regards the hearing of confessions, assistance at marriage and the functions which are reserved to the pastor by law, the jurisdiction is delegated, but in all other affairs it is ordinary jurisdiction.

However, the majority of authors claim that the assistant has merely delegated jurisdiction.[23] These authors state that their opinion is certain, and some of them base their arguments on a private response of the Pontifical Commission.[24] The Pontifical Commission was asked: "Since according to canon 476, § 6, a parochial assistant is bound by virtue of his office to take the place of the pastor and to assist him in all the work of the parish, it is asked: Whether he can validly assist at marriages and delegate others to assist at the same, if it does not appear from the diocesan statutes nor from the letters of the ordinary, nor from his commission from the pastor, that any limitation of his rights has been imposed." The reply of the president of the Commission was: "In the negative to both." [25] This

[21] Cf. can. 474.

[22] *Das Personenrecht des Codex Iuris Canonici* (Paderborn, 1924), p. 228.

[23] De Meester, *Juris canonici et juris canonico-civilis compendium* (3 vols. in 4, Brugis, 1921-1928), II, n. 881, 1; Jone, *Gesetzbuch des kanonischen Rechtes,* I, 380; Vermeersch-Creusen, *Epitome,* I, n. 571; Prümmer, *Manuale Iuris Canonici* (6. ed., quam curavit Engelbertus M. Münch, Friburgi Brisgoviae: Herder & Co., 1933), p. 224; De Smet, "Recentiores Variationes in re matrimoniali,"—*Ephemerides Theologicae Lovaniensis,* I (1924), 560; Rettenbacher, "Der Kooperator nach dem neuen Codex Iuris,"—*Theol.-prakt. Quartalschrift,* LXXII (1919), 338; Fanfani, *De Iure Parochorum* (editio altera, Taurini-Romae: Marietti, 1936), n. 473. Fanfani changed his opinion, for in the first edition of his work he claimed that the assistant has ordinary jurisdiction.

[24] Pont. Comm. Intr., 13 sept. 1933—*Irish Ecclesiastical Record,* XXXXVI (1933), 637.

[25] Cf. Bouscaren, *Canon Law Digest,* II, 153.

answer would be incongruous if the assistant had ordinary jurisdiction. Thus, it must be concluded that the assistant cannot grant a decree of nullity, even in the absence of the pastor, unless he has been delegated or unless he is the substitute.

From the canonical point of view all persons enumerated in this chapter, with the exception of the major religious superior, the official, and the parochial assistant, are competent to act in the cases of nullity of a marriage when the parties failed to observe the form. This is the law, but the practice and custom are different. From a practical point of view it is much better to submit these cases to the diocesan curia, and to have either the bishop himself or the vicar general grant the decree of nullity after the pastor has made the preliminary investigations. This simplifies the matter of keeping a proper record of all these cases. Inquiries are directed to the chancery office of the diocese. It would require much writing back and forth, if each astor were to act in these cases.

If a marriage is not only evidently null because of defect of form, but also invalid by reason of existence of a diriment impediment, the question will arise as to what process should be followed, namely, the administrative process as outlined in Article 231 of the Instruction of 1936, or the summary process according to the norms of canon 1990? Under these circumstances the easier procedure may be followed, namely, to declare the marriage null because the parties failed to observe the form of marriage. This, however, presupposes that the nullity of the marriage has been established convincingly and all prudent doubt been removed.

If a Catholic party petitions the ordinary for a declaration of the nullity of the marriage, and the investigation shows that the party contracted marriage outside the Church not only once, but twice or three times, and each time with different persons, is the ordinary competent to grant the decree of nullity? Certainly, for the accumulation of violations of the law does not restrict or remove the jurisdiction of the ordinary.

CHAPTER VI

PROOFS AND PROCEDURE

Article 231, § 1, states: "*. . . ad hoc ut constet de horum statu libero, neque iudiciales sollemnitates requiruntur, neque interventus defensoris vinculi: sed hi casus solvendi sunt ab Ordinario ipso, vel a parocho, consulto Ordinario, in praevia investigatione ad matrimonii celebration, de qua in can. 1019 sqq.*"

IF a person, after having attempted a civil marriage or a marriage before a non-Catholic minister, intends to contract a marriage according to the rite of the Church, the following facts must be ascertained in order to establish the free status of the person:

a. That the attempted marriage before the civil official or non-Catholic minister was really not contracted according to the rite of the Church, and that no convalidation of the marriage has ever been obtained;

b. That the parties were bound to observe the form, and the inquiry is important especially if they were born of apostates, of non-Catholics, or of a mixed marriage.

1. The Petition

The petition is a brief outline of the facts of the case, asking the competent ecclesiastical authority to consider the case and to grant a decree of nullity, if from the documents submitted it is evident that the marriage has been contracted outside the Church.[1]

While the statement of facts should be brief, it should nevertheless be complete. If the facts are stated incompletely, such action can readily occasion a delay in the procedure. The petition must contain the name of the person who seeks the decree of nullity. It must state whether the person is a Catholic, an apostate, a baptized non-Catholic, or unbaptized. It should state that the person was

[1] Cf. Appendix, Form n. 7.

bound to observe the form, either *per se* or by virtue of the principle: *Pars ligata communicat alteri suum ligamen.* The petition must state in what city or county and in what state the person obtained a civil license to marry. Then the petition must give the name of the person with whom the marriage was contracted outside the Church, and it must state whether this person was a Catholic, an apostate, a baptized non-Catholic, or unbaptized. The petition must include the date of the attempted marriage, where it was contracted, and before whom it was contracted. Furthermore, it should state whether or not a civil divorce or annulment has been obtained. If it has been obtained, the place, date and the reasons for the divorce should be given.

The petitioner should state the claim that his marriage is null and void because of defect of form and that a decree of nullity is sought from the proper ecclesiastical authority.

The petition should be addressed to the bishop or pastor in whose territory the party has a domicile or quasi-domicile, or in cases of *vagi* to the bishop or pastor of the territory where the party actually resides. The petition should list all the documents and proofs that are submitted by the party. The petitioner must sign the petition, giving place and date on the bottom of it. The petition should bear the signature of the pastor or priest who aided the person in the case. The fee for the chancery expenses should be enclosed with the petition.[2] If the parties are unable to defray the expenses, this should be indicated on the petition by the notation: *in forma pauperum.*

If both parties petition for a decree of nullity, it is proper to have both parties write a petition. This is not absolutely necessary, but it is helpful in order to exclude all possible collusion. If, for example, one party states that the marriage was contracted before a civil official, but the other party claims that the marriage ceremony was performed by a non-Catholic minister, a closer investigation into the case will be necessary to find out what really did happen. It is possible that the parties are then seeking to hide something which could point favorably to the validity of the marriage. Of course, only one set of documents is necessary to accompany these petitions.

If the person is unable to write, the priest who assists the party

[2] Cf. *infra,* Chap. VII.

should write the petition, but he should not sign it with the petitioner's name. Under these circumstances the petitioner should sign the petition with a mark such as an "X," but two persons should be called upon to witness this mark, and to sign their names under the petitioner's mark.

In order to simplify the whole procedure a filled out questionnaire should be attached to the petition. The questionnaire consists of a number of general questions, asking about the name, place of birth, occupation, etc., of the petitioner, and a number of special questions pertaining directly to the case. The parties should answer these questions under oath.

2. Establishment of the Free Status

Before the decree of nullity can be granted, and the party be permitted to contract a marriage, it must be established that the party is free. It is not necessary to determine here that the party is free to contract licitly and validly a marriage with the other person, for that belongs to the prenuptial investigation as it is outlined in canons 1019 ff. But it must be determined that the party is free to marry insofar as the previous marriage entered into before a civil official or non-Catholic minister was null. There is a similarity between this investigation and the prenuptial investigation, insofar as both procedures are merely administrative and not judicial; and both the investigation concerning the free status of the parties and the prenuptial investigation require practically the same documents. This is the chief reason for which Article 231 of the Instruction of 1936 points to the investigation preparatory to the celebration of marriage as indicated in canon 1019 and the subsequent canons.

Inasmuch as the article states: ". . . ad hoc ut constet de statu libero. . .," it is quite evident that it is not sufficient that there be merely some probability for the free status of the person. This free status must be determined with moral certainty, so that every prudent doubt is excluded. The moral certainty is reached by using all the available means which according to the circumstances of the case are necessary and can be applied in order to prove the free status of the parties. Such means of proof are documents, *e. g.*, the baptismal record of the Catholic party, or affidavits of trustworthy Catholics.

In the case of danger of death on the side of one or both of the parties, or in other extreme cases, *e. g.*, uncertainty of departure during the time of mobilization, when it is impossible to obtain other documents, the sworn statement of the parties suffices. Such a case may occur when a Catholic has attempted marriage with a non-Catholic before a civil official. After a few years they obtain a civil divorce, and the Catholic, who was certainly bound to observe the form, attempts a new marriage with a baptized non-Catholic before a non-Catholic minister. The Catholic party is now in danger of death and calls for a priest. In the course of conversation the Catholic party reveals that he had attempted a marriage previously with a non-Catholic before a civil official, but he wishes to have the second attempted marriage rectified. The time does not permit the pastor to make a close investigation in the case to determine that the first attempted marriage was really null and void. Under these circumstances the sworn statement of the party would suffice. However, even under these circumstances one should not neglect to use all means of proof that are available, if the time permits it.[8]

In order to determine the free status of the parties in regard to the declaration of the nullity of a marriage contracted outside the Church, the following documents and factors shall be considered and discussed:

a. The baptismal certificate of the Catholic party;
b. The record of Confirmation or first Holy Communion;
c. Proof of Catholic education;
d. Certified copy of the marriage record;
e. Record of civil divorce or annulment;
f. Affidavits from at least two trustworthy Catholic persons testifying that the marriage was never rectified;
g. Report of search in the files of chancery offices;
h. The supplementary oath.

[8] Cf. Schönsteiner, *Grundriss des kirchlichen Eherechts* (2. ed., Wien: Verlag der Buchhandlung Ludwig Auer, 1937), p. 137.

It is quite evident that not all of these documents and factors are called for in every case in order to obtain a decree of nullity. Some cases require a greater number of documents than others, depending on the fact whether the limited number of documents submitted is sufficient to afford the requisite moral certainty that the marriage is null.

a. *Baptismal Certificate of the Catholic Party.*

A baptismal certificate is an authentic document testifying that the person mentioned therein has received the sacrament of baptism according to the rite of the Catholic Church.[4] Before a declaration of nullity can be granted, the petitioner must produce the baptismal certificate of the Catholic party. The baptismal certificate is absolutely necessary in order to show that the person was baptized in the Catholic Church, and thus was subject to the law on the form of marriage. If both of the parties who attempted to contract a marriage outside the Church are Catholics and petition for a decree of nullity, both must normally furnish their baptismal records. However, the baptismal record of one is surely enough for moral certainty. In order to have an authentic copy of the baptismal record, the certificate must be signed by the pastor or some other authorized person of the place where the party was baptized, and it must bear the official seal of the parish. Inasmuch as the baptismal record should indicate whether or not the marriage attempted by the parties had ever been rectified by a simple convalidation or sanation, the baptismal certificate should be of recent date. In any event, a baptismal record should never be older than six months.[5] If the Catholic party is a convert to the Catholic Faith, but baptism was not conferred at the time of the conversion because it was evident that baptism had already been conferred validly, the pastor of the place of conversion must issue an authentic document testifying to the fact of the conversion of the party. If it is revealed that the party, though validly baptized previously, did not become a convert to the Faith until after the marriage with the non-Catholic had been contracted before a

[4] Cf. Appendix, Form n. 1.

[5] S. C. de Sacramentis, instr. 29 iun. 1941, n. 4 c.—*The Jurist*, II (1942), supplement.

civil official or a non-Catholic minister, it is quite obvious that a decree of nullity cannot be granted, because the party was not subject to the canonical form of marriage at the time the marriage was contracted. But once the party was formally received into the Church, the obligation to observe the juridical form of marriage was incumbent on the person. Therefore, if baptism was not administered either absolutely or conditionally at the time of the formal conversion, an authentic document testifying to the fact of conversion will be required.

Canon 1021 states in part: ". . . nisi baptismus collatus fuerit in ipso suo territorio, parochus exigat baptismi testimonium." Now, it may happen that it is impossible to obtain a baptismal certificate, because the records were destroyed when the rectory or church was destroyed by fire, or because one can not get in touch with the place where the party was baptized, as for example during war-time. A person, for example, who from infancy on was considered a Catholic, and was admitted to the sacraments of penance, Holy Eucharist, and confirmation, may find it now impossible to obtain a certificate of his baptism. Especially in the cases of illegitimate children it is not always easy to obtain a certificate of baptism. Under what name was the child entered in the baptismal record? Was the entry made under the name of the mother or father? Perhaps the name of the child was merely entered as the child of unknown parents.[6]

The question then arises, whether the baptismal certificate is absolutely necessary under these circumstances. The answer is No, for the fact of baptism can be proved through other means, *e. g.*, through a trustworthy witness, such as the mother of the child or the sponsors, or the person himself will be able to testify to the fact of his baptism provided that the person was baptized as an adult.[7] However, such a sworn statement will not be sufficient in a judicial trial.[8]

[6] Cf. can. 777, § 2.

[7] Can. 779: "Ad collatum baptismum comprobandum, si nemini fiat praeiudicium, satis est unus testis omni exceptione maior, vel ipsius baptizati iusiurandum, si ipse in adulta aetate baptismum receperit."

[8] Can. 1791, § 1: "Unius testis depositio plenam fidem non facit, nisi sit testis qualificatus qui deponat de rebus ex officio gestis." Cf. Willet, *The*

A presumption of law for the reception of baptism attends the authentic proof that the person received first Holy Communion and the sacrament of confirmation. The baptismal certificate is not absolutely necessary to contract a marriage. In favor of the reception of baptism is the fact that the person was born of Catholic parents and was always regarded as a Catholic.[9]

If after due investigation there remains a prudent doubt, and if that doubt is not solved in a judicial trial, namely, whether the party was baptized, then there will remain the same kind of doubt as to whether the marriage attempted by the party before the civil official or non-Catholic minister was really null and void. The case is such that the doubt concerning the baptism of the party cannot be settled one way or another. If the baptism was conferred, the attempted marriage is null; but if the baptism was not conferred, the attempted marriage is certainly valid, even though it was contracted outside the Church, for the party, not being subject to the laws of the Church, was correspondingly not obliged to observe the canonical form. Under these circumstances the case cannot be settled by either the ordinary, the official or the pastor, but should be sent to the Holy See for settlement. A case of this nature, which was sent to the Sacred Penitentiary for settlement, was taken care of by the Holy See through the granting of a dissolution of the natural bond of marriage *ad cautelam*. The principle, "In dubio standum est pro valore matrimonii,"[10] must be applied in a doubt as given above, if it is to be presumed that the party was not bound to observe the form, for if the party was not obliged to observe the form, then the marriage contracted before a civil official or a non-Catholic minister had the appearance or aspect of a true marriage. But if the validity of the baptism of the party is to be presumed, and therefore the party was obliged to observe the canonical form of marriage, then the principle cannot be applied, for this principle presumes that there is at least the appearance or the semblance of a true marriage.

Probative Value of Documents in Ecclesiastical Trials, The Catholic University of America Canon Law Studies, n. 171 (Washington, D. C.: The Catholic University of America Press, 1942).

[9] S. C. S. Off. (Savannah), 1 aug. 1883—*Fontes*, n. 1083.

[10] Cf. can. 1014.

The validity of baptism, therefore, may be questioned on two grounds, namely, a doubt may arise as to the fact of its actual administration (*dubium dubio facti*), or its administration being certain, there may be a doubt whether the proper matter and form were used (*dubium dubio iuris*). It is generally admitted that either of these doubts is sufficient to invest the baptism with a presumptive validity in relation to marriage,[11] and the same kind of validity would be communicated to the marriage contracted in such doubts.[12]

If in a case *ad matrimonium contrahendum* there exists a prudent doubt either about the fact of the reception of the sacrament of baptism or about the validity of the baptism conferred, the party is obliged to be baptized *sub conditione* before the Catholic party may be permitted to marry.[13] If the party refuses to be baptized *sub conditione* the ordinary by virtue of canon 15 [14] can grant a dispensation from mixed religion (*ad cautelam*) in order to prepare the way for a valid marriage.[15]

b. *Record of Confirmation or First Holy Communion*

A record of confirmation is an authentic document testifying that the person named therein has received the sacrament of confirmation in accordance with the rite of the Catholic Church.[16] The record of confirmation is required before a decree of nullity can be granted in order to show the Catholic education of the party involved in the case of nullity. Therefore a record of confirmation is only then

[11] Gasparri, *De Matrimonio,* n. 603.

[12] Petrovits, *The New Church Law on Matrimony* (2. ed., Philadelphia: John Joseph McVey, 1926), pp. 174-175.

[13] Can. 732, § 2: "Si vero prudens dubium exsistat num revera vel num valide collata fuerint, sub conditione iterum conferantur." Compare this with canon 737, § 1: "Baptismus, Sacramentorum ianua ac fundamentum, omnibus in re vel saltem in voto necessarius ad salutem, valide non confertur, nisi per ablutionem aquae verae et naturalis cum praescripta verborum forma."

[14] "Leges, etiam irritantes et inhabilitantes, in dubio iuris non urgent; in dubio autem facti potest Ordinarius in eis dispensare, dummodo agatur de legibus in quibus Romanus Pontifex dispensare solet."

[15] Cf. Oesterle, "Ehe ohne Taufschein,"—*Theol.-prakt. Quartalschrift,* XIIIC (1940), 312-313.

[16] Cf. Appendix, Form n. 2.

necessary, when the Catholic education of the party must be proved. The record must be obtained if the party was born of non-Catholic parents or of a mixed marriage, for it is possible that, if the Catholic party was only baptized in the Catholic Church, but reared in heresy and schism, he or she would not be subject to the canonical form of marriage. If the child was confirmed, that fact is sufficient proof to show that the child received a Catholic education after having reached the age of reason.

Now, it is customary in some countries, *e. g.*, in Mexico, and even among the Mexican people residing in the United States, that the children are confirmed soon after baptism, or at a very early age. The child is confirmed before it has reached the age of reason, and hence before it has received proper Catholic education. Under these circumstances it is quite evident that the fact of the administration of the sacrament of confirmation does not constitute a proof for the Catholic education of the child. The certificate of confirmation can not be accepted as a proof that the Catholic party was subject to the canonical form of marriage, even though he or she was born of non-Catholic parents or of a mixed marriage and was also baptized in the Catholic Church. But in the absence of a baptismal record the certificate of confirmation can be accepted as a proof for the fact that baptism was conferred, for no one can receive confirmation without having first been baptized.

If a confirmation certificate cannot be obtained, or if it is useless to obtain one, since it would not prove the Catholic education of the party inasmuch as the party was confirmed when an infant, then a certificate must be obtained from the pastor of the parish where the child received its first Holy Communion.[17] For, if it can be shown that the party received first Holy Communion, then the proof of the Catholic education of the party has been established. Furthermore, outside of the case of danger of death it is required that the children have an appreciably full knowledge of the Catholic doctrine when they are being prepared for the reception of their first Holy Communion.[18]

[17] Cf. Appendix, Form n. 3.

[18] Can. 854, § 3: "Extra mortis periculum plenior cognitio doctrinae christianae et accuratior praeparatio merito exigitur. . . ."

c. *Proof of Catholic Education*

The mere learning by rote of certain Catholic prayers is of itself not the equivalent of even a rudimentary Catholic education. Therefore the fact of a Catholic education cannot be determined solely by the amount of knowledge that a person has concerning the Christian doctrine; it must be determined in addition by the actual training that the person has received. If the fact of a Catholic education were determined solely by the amount of knowledge that is had regarding Christian doctrine, then a child of a mixed marriage, though instructed for many years in the Catholic Faith, would never be bound when it grows up to observe the canonical form of marriage, if in spite of the many years of training it did not have more than a rudimentary knowledge of the essentials of the Christian Faith.

It is a presumption of law that a child reaches the use of reason at the age of seven.[19] This presumption prevails unless it can be shown that the child had reached the use of reason before the age of seven. Now, the normal child enters school at the age of six. The first year of school can hardly be considered, even though the child received a few catechism instructions, for the child has not as yet reached the age of reason. But after the child has reached the age of reason, it seems that two years of religious instruction, either in school at regular times, or at home privately, would constitute the minimum for a Catholic education. Therefore, if in the absence of a record of first Holy Communion or confirmation it is ascertained that the child received religious instructions for two years after having reached the age of reason, it is very safe to state that this child received a Catholic education, and hence was bound in later life to observe the canonical form of marriage.

It may happen in certain cases that the child received baptism and was sent to a Catholic school, but that, when the child was about nine years old, the Catholic parent who had supervised the Catholic education of the child died. Immediately upon the parent's death the non-Catholic spouse took the child out of the Catholic school and began a systematic training of the child in heresy, schism or infi-

[19] Cf. can. 88.

delity. The child never received first Holy Communion nor the sacrament of confirmation. Therefore it is impossible to obtain these documents in order to prove the Catholic education of the child. These facts are revealed when the party petitions the proper ecclesiastical superior for a declaration of nullity because of defect of proper canonical form. Under these circumstances it is necessary to obtain a written statement from the pastor or principal in charge of the Catholic school which the party attended up to the time of the death of the Catholic parent. This letter must certify that the child attended the Catholic school and received catechism instructions. If the party attended a public school, then the pastor in whose parish the party resided as a child must testify that the child received proper instructions in Christian doctrine.[20]

In some places the pastor visits the public school after the regular class hours several times during the week; in other places the pastor instructs the children in church at appointed hours during the week. If it is ascertained that the child never attended the instructions in Christian doctrine, was never confirmed, and never received first Holy Communion, the exemption as stated in canon 1099, § 2, is applicable, even thought the party knows a number of prayers, such as the Our Father and the Hail Mary, which he had been taught by the Catholic parent. However, if the party has been instructed in the Faith by the Catholic parent, although privately, the exemption of canon 1099, § 2, cannot be applied. Whether or not the party has been instructed privately by the Catholic parent can perhaps be gathered from the amount of knowledge that the person has concerning the Christian doctrine.

Now, a person could claim that his religious instruction did not cover the chapter on marriage, and thus he did not know that there was a prescribed juridical form for marriage. This, however, would be no excuse to justify his being included in the exemption of canon 1099, § 2. The fact of a Catholic education is not determined by the amount of knowledge that a person has concerning the Christian doctrine; it must be determined by the actual training that the person has received.

[20] Cf. Appendix, Form n. 4.

d. Certified Copy of Marriage Record

This is a copy of the official testimonial of the contracted marriage issued by the county clerk, or by some other official person of the county or the State in which the persons attempted to contract the marriage either before a civil official or in the presence of a non-Catholic minister. The marriage record generally indicates whether the marriage ceremony was performed by a civil official or by a minister of religion. If the parties attempted to contract a marriage before a minister of religion or a civil official, most of the states require that the minister or civil official after having performed the marriage ceremony return the license to the county clerk properly signed by the officiant of the marriage. This marriage record is required to show that the parties actually contracted a marriage outside the Church, and that they were not merely living in concubinage.

At times it may not be possible to obtain a copy of the civil marriage record, but the parties have a record of their civil divorce or annulment. The obtaining of a civil marriage record must be dispensed with, if it is difficult to obtain it. It would not be correct to make it a general rule and to state that, as long as the parties produce the decree of civil divorce or annulment, the marriage record is not required, for the decree of a civil divorce does not necessarily indicate that the parties were married civilly. Their sworn statement of the facts of the alleged marriage is all that the courts require in divorce proceedings. The courts do not require a copy of the marriage record. The parties should be asked why they cannot obtain the record of their civil marriage. At times it is possible that the parties are trying to conceal some vital information, since the marriage record will give the name of the officiant, *e. g.*, Rev. N. N., Pastor of Immaculate Conception Church, or Rev. N. N., Pastor of the First Presbyterian Church, etc. If the Catholic party has attempted more than one civil marriage, then certified copies of the records of all the marriages contracted outside the Church must be obtained.

e. Record of Civil Divorce or Annulment

The civil annulment is a decree, issued by the civil court after the hearing of the case, declaring that the civil marriage of the parties is null and void, because of the reasons alleged by the plaintiff. A civil divorce is a decree severing the bond of a civilly valid marriage. According to the civil law the parties are usually free after such a decree to contract a new marriage, frequently with certain restrictions as to time and persons. In a few states they are not permitted to marry after a decree of divorce.[21]

In order to grant a declaration of nullity because of the defect of canonical form, a civil divorce or annulment is not absolutely necessary. In other words, the proper ecclesiastical authority could grant a decree of nullity even though the parties had not been divorced in accordance with civil law. The statutes of some States provide that the parties cannot obtain a divorce decree unless they have resided in a certain territory for a determined length of time. Under these circumstances the parties could be granted a decree of nullity before they have obtained a civil divorce. The civil divorce is only necessary in order to safeguard the civil effects of the civil marriage, and to protect the parties themselves.[22] If, for example, the ecclesiastical authority granted a decree of nullity before the parties had obtained a civil divorce or annulment, and the parties then married again, the State could prosecute them for the crime of bigamy. As far as the State is concerned, as long as the parties to a civilly valid marriage have not obtained a civil divorce, they are to be regarded as still married. Therefore, if they attempt a second marriage they are guilty of bigamy, unless the first marriage has been dissolved by the State.

An ecclesiastical decree of nullity can be issued also before a civil interlocutory decree of divorce has become final.

If the ecclesiastical authority for certain reasons grants a decree of nullity before the parties have obtained a civil divorce or before the civil interlocutory decree of divorce has become final, they should be admonished that they should not contract a new marriage until

[21] Alford, *Jus Matrimoniale Comparatum*, pp. 163-164.

[22] Willett (*The Probative Value of Documents in Ecclesiastical Trials*, p. 87) writes as follows: "The general practice of diocesan courts which requires a civil divorce certificate in cases of declaration of nullity . . . is not indeed demanded by the Code, but is a wise procedure which should be followed to avoid conflict with the civil law."

they have obtained the civil divorce or until the civil interlocutory decree of divorce has become final in view of its beneficial civil consequences. If the parties have obtained more than one civil divorce inasmuch as they contracted more than one civil marriage, they should be requested to submit all the divorce certificates.

f. Affidavits from at Least Two Trustworthy Catholics Testifying That the Marriage Was Never Rectified

The affidavit is a written declaration or statement confirmed either by oath or by a solemn affirmation. An affidavit merely certifies that a specific person made a solemn affirmation confirmed by oath before a duly qualified notary public at a certain time. In the opinion of the Sacred Roman Rota, declarations and affirmations contained in affidavits do not constitute full proof in ecclesiastical courts; but they do give corroborative force to extant proof. Moreover, since they are public documents when made before public notaries, they afford certainty about those things which are directly and primarily affirmed.[23] Hence the affidavit in question is a document testifying to the fact that the attempted marriage of the parties in the case has never been rectified. Therefore it is necessary that the person who signs the affidavit must have known the parties from the time that they attempted to contract the marriage either before a civil official or a non-Catholic minister. The person who signs the affidavit must be a trustworthy Catholic. He must be a practical Catholic who is well acquainted with the teachings of the Church. Hence all excommunicated persons, or persons who are indifferent in the practice of their Faith, must be excluded.

[23] S. R. R., *Nullitas matrimonii,* 5 iun. 1926, *coram R. P. D. Josepho Florczak,* dec. XXIV, n. 7: "Depositiones coram iudice ecclesiastico factae plene confirmantur ab iis quae coram notario civili sub iuramento declaraverunt. Hae declarationes enim, etsi perfectam probationem efficere nequeant, cum non constituant iudiciales testificationes iuxta can. 1754 et seqq., eoque magis quod in iis conficiendis defuerat vinculi defensor, cuius praesentia requiritur ad normam canonis 1587,' valorem tamen adminiculativum habent. Prout enim a notario publico rite confectae fuerunt secundum Statuum Foederatorum Americae Septentrionalis leges, documenta publica constituunt, ideoque ex can. 1816 'fidem faciunt de iis quae directe et principaliter in eisdem affirmantur.' " —*S. R. R. Dec.,* XVIII (1926), 195. Cf. Willett, *op. cit.,* pp. 85-86.

The best method of securing the affidavit is to have it in the form of questions and answers.[24] The questionnaire should begin with the fact that the person having acknowledged the nature and sanctity of an oath, and being duly sworn, deposes as follows, etc. The questionnaire should be divided into two sections: the section of general questions and the section of special questions. The general questions should inquire for the name of the affiant, his age, religion, address, etc.; the special questions should deal directly with the matter in hand. It should be determined whether the person signing the affidavit knows the petitioner or respondent, whether the affiant and the petitioner or the respondent are related, whether the petitioner or the respondent were ever married or ever attempted marriage, and if so, by whom, where and when, and whether this marriage was ever rectified in the Church, etc.

After having given the answers, the person should read the deposition, or at least it should be read to the person by the one who asked the questions, and the affiant should be asked whether he or she wishes to add, suppress or change anything from the written deposition contained in the affidavit. Then the person signs the affidavit, and the priest acting as notary or any public notary who recorded the testimony puts his signature below the signature of the affiant. If the person cannot write, then two persons must be called upon to witness the mark that the person places under the testimony. Mention of the date and place must always be affixed to the document, and the document must carry the official seal of the notary.

g. *Report of Search in the Files of Chancery Offices*

Some diocesan curias have adopted the practice of instituting a search in the files of the chancery office of the diocese where the parties lived after the attempted marriage. It can easily be seen that if the parties resided in the same diocese from the time they attempted to contract a marriage outside the Church until they petition the ecclesiastical authority for a declaration of nullity, this search does not have to be made, for the diocesan files should show whether or not a simple convalidation or a sanation was ever granted in the

[24] Cf. Appendix, Form n. 6.

case. But the question arises whether this search in the files of the chancery offices is at all necessary and practical if the parties resided in more than one diocese from the time they attempted to contract the marriage until they petitioned the Church for a decree of nullity regarding it.

Such a search is neither necessary nor practical, for if the parties have a baptismal certificate of recent date, the record should show whether or not the marriage was ever rectified. According to canon 1103, § 2, the parish priest is to note in the book of baptisms the fact that the married person contracted marriage on a given date in his parish. If the married person was baptized elsewhere, the parish priest who has assisted at the marriage is to send notice of the marriage, either directly or through the episcopal curia, to the parish priest of the place where the person was baptized, in order that the marriage may be inscribed in the book of baptisms. This inscription may be inserted by means of a simple marginal note written alongside the name of the parties in the book of baptisms. If this law is complied with as strictly as circumstances permit, the inquiry as to the free status of the parties before marriage will be greatly facilitated and many abuses will be prevented. To find out whether the parties are bound by a marital contract it will suffice to consult the baptismal register, or the baptismal certificate. The marriage registers cannot very often be consulted. Marriage publicly celebrated in one place can remain unknown in another, and if it is entered in only one book of marriages, it is easy to conceal the fact of marriage if it is recorded in a remote district. But if the record of all the possible marriages validly contracted by a man is kept together with the record of his baptism, then the record of the marriages will be as easily traceable as the record of baptism.[25]

It is absolutely necessary that the baptismal record be of recent date, and the pastor or the one who assists the parties in obtaining the necessary documents should not accept a record that was issued at a time when the parties were living in the territory of another diocese, for the parties could have obtained a simple convalidation or a sanation in the meantime, which would not be recorded on their

[25] Cf. Ayrinhac, *Marriage Legislation*, pp. 275-280.

old baptismal record. If, for example, the parties have resided for three months in the diocese in which they apply for the declaration of nullity, then the baptismal record should not be older than three months.

Another reason why a search in the files of the chancery offices is futile is that, if the parties intend to perjure themselves, they will certainly not mention the place where the marriage was actually rectified. If, for example, the parties resided in St. Louis and New York and then moved to Washington, where they now apply for a declaration of nullity, and they are calculatingly determined to obtain the declaration of nullity, they will certainly not mention that they lived in New York for a certain length of time, if in New York the marriage had actually been rectified. Therefore, not knowing that the parties resided in New York, because they did not reveal this information, the priest will write to the chancery office in St. Louis. Upon investigation in the files the chancery office at St. Louis will reply that the files do not show that a simple convalidation or sanation has ever been granted in the case. In this case it is quite evident that the search in the files was absolutely useless, for the parties, being quite willing to perjure themselves, concealed the fact that at one time they resided in St. Louis.

Some diocesan curias require that a search be instituted if any doubt remains. But what doubt could remain, if the parties, under oath, claim that the marriage was never rectified, and if this testimony is confirmed by the affidavits of two trustworthy Catholics?

It would be interesting to know how many cases were actually found in the files of the chancery offices upon request to institute a search. If the parties answer truthfully the questions proposed to them, there is no reason to institute a search; and if the parties do not answer the questions truthfully, a search will be futile, for if the parties have made up their minds to lie about one thing, they certainly will not feel any remorse of conscience to conceal the other thing. If they answer the question whether their marriage has ever been rectified in the negative, they certainly will not mention the place where the marriage actually has been rectified.

h. The Supplementary Oath

If the case is partly but not sufficiently proved, and no further corroboration for the incomplete proofs is available, then the one handling the case may order or admit a sworn statement to supplement the case.[26] Thus the supplementary oath may be admitted to determine the free status of the parties when no proof is available. The Holy Office speaks of the supplementary oath as proof of the free status of the parties when all other proofs are wanting.[27] Lega-Bartoccetti make a distinction between matrimonial cases that treat of marriage to be dissolved (*de matrimonio dissolvendo*) and matrimonial cases that treat of marriages to be contracted (*de nuptiis contrahendis*).[28] In the former cases the supplementary oath cannot be admitted; but in the latter cases, if all other proofs are wanting, the supplementary oath may be admitted to supplement the case.

From a private response of the S. Congregation of the Sacraments it is evident that the S. Congregation considers that the Code by reason of canons 1829 and 1830, § 1, grants to ordinaries the faculty to administer the supplementry oath as a means of ascertaining the freedom of the parties.[29]

Therefore, if the proper ecclesiastical authority hesitates to grant a decree of nullity because of defect of canonical form by reason of insufficient proof, the parties should be asked to take the supplementary oath. This is true if there is no evidence that the marriage was rectified. If such evidence exists, a strictly judicial process is necessary. The supplementary oath should supply whatever evidence is lacking in the case. If, for example, two trustworthy Catholics cannot be called upon to sign an affidavit that the marriage has never been rectified either by simple convalidation or by means of a sana-

[26] Wanenmacher, *Canonical Evidence in Marriage Cases* (Philadelphia, Pa.: Dolphin Press, 1935), p. 365.

[27] S. C. S. Off. (ad Deleg. Ap. Aegypt.), 13 ian. 1869—*Fontes*, n. 1008.

[28] Lega, *Commentarius in Iudicia Ecclesiastica iuxta Codicem Iuris Canonici* (curante Victorio Bartoccetti, 3 vols., Romae: Anonima Libraria Cattolica Italiana, 1938-1941), II, 831.

[29] Bouscaren, *Canon Law Digest, Supplement—1941*, pp. 121-122, under can. 1023.

tion, then the parties in the case should be requested to take a supplementary oath to the same effect, namely, that the attempted marriage has never been rectified.[80]

3. The Decree of Nullity

After all the documents have been submitted to prove that the parties neglected to observe the canonical form of marriage, the competent ecclesiastical authority issues a decree of nullity. The decree should state the name of the parties to whom the declaration is granted. It should mention the cause for the nullity of the marriage, namely, the defect of form; and it should bear the signature of the one granting the declaration of nullity. The document should state when and where the decree was granted, and it should also bear the signature of a notary.[81]

The decree of nullity should preferably be written in Latin in order to give the document that universality which it would not have if it were drawn up in the vernacular. The names of the parties should be written accurately, but a slight mistake in the spelling of the names would not invalidate the decree.[82] It is quite obvious that if the cause for the nullity of the marriage, namely, the lack of the proper canonical form, does not correspond to actual fact at the time the decree is issued, the decree is null and void.

The original copy of the decree is not given to the petitioner or the respondent, but is sent to the pastor of the petitioner or to the priest who assisted the petitioner in the case, for the decree must be kept in the archives of the parish.[83] The pastor, upon receipt of the decree, must inform the petitioner of the declaration of nullity. The pastor must send a proper notice to the place of baptism of the Catholic party, informing the pastor of the place of baptism that a decree of nullity has been obtained by the party, in order that this pastor may make a note of it in the baptismal register. This is only

[80] Cf. Appendix, Form n. 5.

[81] Cf. Appendix, Form n. 9.

[82] Cf. can. 47.

[83] Cf. Appendix, Form n. 10.

necessary if there has been the semblance of a marriage, and the case has gone through an ordinary procedure.[84]

Together with the decree of nullity all legal papers, such as the record of the civil marriage, the civil divorce decree, etc., should be sent to the one who submitted the case in the name of the petitioner. The legal documents submitted are returned by him to the petitioner. But the chancery office should keep a memorandum of the case, as well as the petition itself. This memorandum must give the names of the parties in the case, placing the name of the petitioner before the name of the respondent, and thus filing the memorandum under the name of the petitioner; it must state when the attempted marriage was contracted and before whom the parties exchanged their consent; furthermore, it must give the date when the decree was issued and by whom it was granted. The memorandum should also enumerate the list of documents that were submitted in the case.[85]

Upon receipt of the notice that a declaration of nullity has been granted, the parties do not have to wait a certain period of time before they may be allowed to contract a new marriage in accordance with the canonical requirements. But inasmuch as the decree of nullity is an assurance of the free status of the parties, they may enter a new marriage immediately. If the parties are already living in a new union, this may be rectified immediately. If the parties did not obtain a civil divorce, because the civil law required that they reside in a certain territory for a determined length of time before petitioning for a divorce, the parties must be advised to obtain a civil divorce before they contract a new marriage, otherwise the State will prosecute them for the crime of bigamy. It should be pointed out to the parties that the declaration of nullity granted to them by the ecclesiastical superior is not accorded any civil effect whatsoever.

To summarize this chapter: If a case of evident defect of form comes to the attention of the pastor, he should have the party or the parties write up the case in the form of a petition. Then the pastor should ask proper questions such as are attached by the authority of the bishop to printed forms for petition. If the party is a Catholic, was born of Catholic parents, and is well known to the pastor himself,

[84] Cf. Appendix, Form n. 11.

[85] Cf. Appendix, Form n. 12.

the pastor must submit the petition, the questionnaire properly filled out, and the following documents: the record of baptism, the civil marriage record and the civil divorce decree. The pastor should not submit the case before he has obtained all documents necessary in the case.

Upon receipt of the case in the offices of the diocesan curia, the case is given a file number. The documents are inspected, and if they seem sufficient, the ordinary signs a decree of nullity. The intervention of the defender of the marriage bond is definitely not necessary. The decree together with the legal documents are returned to the pastor, the petition and questionnaire and the affidavits are kept in the diocesan archives, the decree of nullity is kept in the parish archives, and the legal documents are returned to the parties or party who submitted the case.

If the parties are not known to the pastor, then besides the above mentioned documents the pastor must submit affidavits of at least two trustworthy Catholics, testifying that the marriage was never rectified, or, in the absence of the affidavits, the supplementary oath of the parties themselves will suffice, in the event that the parties resided within the territorial limits of another diocese during the time they lived together as husband and wife.

If the party in the case was born of non-Catholic parents or apostates, or of a mixed marriage, the pastor should submit the petition and the questionnaire, the record of baptism, the civil marriage record, the civil divorce decree, as well as the documents which adequately prove that the parties or party received a Catholic education. These documents are the records of confirmation, of first Holy Communion, and a parochial school record. If the party is not known to the pastor, and if the party has resided in another diocese in which the marriage could have been rectified, the pastor must submit also the affidavits of at least two trustworthy Catholics, or, in the absence of these, the supplementary oath of the party to the effect that the marriage was never rectified. If the ordinary is not satisfied with the documents submitted, additional documents can always be requested.

CHAPTER VII

CASES OF DOUBT

Article 231, § 2: *"Si quod dubium supersit de recensitis conditionibus in § 1, quaestio ordinarii processus tramite definienda est."*

WHENEVER there is a doubt as to the existence of conditions indicated in § 1, a judicial process must be followed. The judicial process consists of a series of acts and solemnities which are prescribed by law for the settlement of questions or the expediting of affairs by public authority.[1]

A doubt exists whenever the juridical form of marriage is vitiated by a substantial defect. The form of marriage has been observed by the parties in accordance with the canon law. The parties did not contract a civil marriage, neither were they married by a non-Catholic minister. Hence there exists at least the appearance of a true marriage, but because of a substantial defect in the form the marriage is null and void. In order to determine whether the substantial defect exists in any given case, the case must be settled according to the norms of a judicial process, and not in an administrative manner.

A fortiori, it follows that a judicial process must be instituted whenever a marriage has been contracted before a priest who only doubtfully enjoyed proper authorization, either ordinary or delegated, or when his authorization had already expired at the time he assisted at the marriage, or when one of the witnesses failed to be present and the priest conducted the ceremonies with the presence of only one witness, or when one of the witnesses did not hear the expression of acceptance from one or both of the parties, or when

[1] Noval, *Commentarium Codicis Iuris Canonici,* I, *De Processibus,* Pars I, *De Iudiciis,* n. 4; Coronata, *Institutiones Iuris Canonici,* III, n. 1086; Augustine, *A Commentary on Canon Law,* VII, 4-6; Vermeersch-Creusen, *Epitome,* III, n. 1; Lega-Bartoccetti, *Commentarius in Iudicia Ecclesiastica,* I, 17-21.

the witness did not notice any signs signifying that consent was exchanged, and thus cannot testify that the parties actually exchanged consent.

The case of doubt mentioned in the above quoted article does include also the case in which it is doubted whether the parties were bound to observe the canonical form of marriage. Article 231, § 2, requires a judicial process when there is a doubt as to the existence of conditions indicated in § 1; in § 1, one of the conditions is whether a party obliged to the form contracted a marriage before a civil official or a non-Catholic minister. Therefore, when there is any doubt about whether the marriage was contracted before a priest or a civil official or a non-Catholic minister, the judicial process is required.

The doubt that is mentioned must be a positive doubt. There must be a tangible reason for regarding the marriage to be null and void, despite the fact that the union has all the appearances of a true and valid union from the standpoint of the parties' compliance with the requisite juridical form. On the other hand, a merely negative doubt obtains when there is present no tangible reason for considering the marriage to be null and void, but merely a lack of evidence for its validity over and above the evidence already inherent in the union as one which has the appearance of a true marriage.

If a case is introduced on the grounds that the priest who performed the marriage ceremonies lacked proper authorization, and that therefore the marriage was null and void, but the investigation shows that the parties were not bound to observe the juridical form of marriage as prescribed by the Church, the marriage would be valid in spite of the fact that the priest lacked authorization, provided that the parties exchanged a true matrimonial consent. The substantial defect in the form does not affect this marriage in any way, because a form cannot be invalidated when it is not a requirement for the validity of the contract.

The question arises whether the process in cases of doubt must be conducted according to the rules of ordinary procedure [2] or according to the rules of the summary procedure.[3]

[2] Cf. cans. 1552, ss.

[3] Cf. cans. 1990 ss.

The list of the cases which may be tried in a summary process is given in canon 1990.[4] This list is exhaustive and not merely demontrative in character.[5]

In a letter of the Apostolic Delegate to the United States, addressed to the bishops of the United States on the handling of marriage cases,[6] it is stated that the list is exhaustive. "It must be remembered that the impediment of age cannot be handled according to the norms of canon 1990, since this impediment is not included in the *taxative* [*sic*] enumeration of the impediments." The letter continues by stating that in the handling of cases which involve the total lack of the juridical form of marriage, as envisaged in article 231 of the Instruction of August 15, 1936, the complete ruling of the second paragraph of the same article must always be strictly observed, namely: *"Si quod dubium supersit de recensitis conditionibus in* § *1, quaestio ordinarii processus tramite definienda est."*

It seems to be the common opinion that the enumeration of cases in canon 1990 is exhaustive; but as regards the handling of cases in which the form has been observed by the parties but in which the form is vitiated by a substantial defect, or cases in which it is doubted whether the parties were bound to observe the canonical form of marriage, or cases in which it is doubted whether the marriage was contracted before a priest or a civil official or a non-Catholic minister, the canonists have different opinions. In order to present a clear picture of the whole controversy, it will prove helpful to outline the differing opinions presented by the different authors.

According to Coronata[7] a long process can easily be avoided, if the case in question is a notorious and evident fact, by applying

[4] Disparity of worship; orders; solemn vow of chastity; existence of a previous bond of marriage; consanguinity; affinity; spiritual relationship.

[5] A list is said to be exhaustive, if the list is complete in such a way that no other cases, although similar to the one enumerated, may be added to it. In brief, the list is complete. On the other hand, a list is said to be demonstrative, if the list cites a few cases which serve as examples, and leaves room for the addition of other cases of the same general nature.

[6] This letter is reproduced in part and may be found in Bouscaren, *Canon Law Digest, Supplement—1941,* p. 193.

[7] *Institutiones Iuris Canonici,* n. 1501.

the norms of canon 1747, which states that notorious facts do not need proof.

Cappello [8] states that if the form has not been neglected completely by the parties, but that there occurred some substantial defect in the form, e. g., that the pastor assisted at the marriage outside the territorial limits of his parish, or that only one person was called upon to witness the marriage, there it at least the appearance of a properly observed form and hence also the appearance of a true marriage. Therefore the validity or invalidity of a marriage must be determined by a judicial process in such a case. But it can be asked, Cappello continues, whether it would not be allowed to enumerate a case of this kind among the excepted cases which are mentioned in canon 1990.: At first glance this must be denied, for clandestinity, which can be found among the excepted cases in the decree of the Holy Office of June 5, 1889, was purposely omitted, so it seems, in canon 1990. The list of cases in canon 1990 is exhaustive. However, this omission from the canon can and must be explained through the fact that such a defect in the form, especially when the defect is manifest and evident, as, for example, when the case reveals the absence of a qualified witness, occurs very rarely; a substantial defect of that nature cannot be proved very easily by certified and authentic documents. If the substantial defect is very evident in a case, the teaching explained above can be followed, and hence the case can be handled as if the form had been neglected completely by the parties, or as if the prescriptions of canon 1990 were applicable for trying the case in a summary process.

Chelodi (1876-1922) [9] asserts that the impediment of age is not listed among the excepted cases; but he also states that, if the existence of the impediment of age as well as the lack of a dispensation can be established without difficulty, it seems that the nullity of the marriage can be declared without an observance of the solemnities of an ordinary process, or at least canon 1747, n. 1, concerning notorious facts, can be applied. As regards the defect of the prescribed form, concerning which canon 1990 is silent, Chelodi says that the following distinction must be made: If the marriage was entered

[8] *De Matrimonio,* III, n. 894.

[9] *Ius Matrimoniale,* n. 180.

into by parties who neglected to observe the form (*e. g.*, by contracting a civil marriage), it is sufficient that the case be settled by the ordinary or by the pastor, the latter having previously consulted the ordinary. The procedure to be followed is the same as the investigation into the free status of the contracting parties. Inasmuch as there is not even the appearance of a marriage, the Church does not consider it as a true marriage. On the contrary, if the form has been observed by the parties, but there exists a substantial defect in the form (*e. g.*, if a priest assisted at the marriage without having the proper delegation), the procedure to be followed has been controverted for a long time. If the substantial defect in the juridical form is quite evident, it seems that the ordinary may proceed as if the form had been neglected completely, or at least the ordinary may proceed according to the norms of canon 1990. However, if there exists a doubt concerning this substantial defect, the ordinary judicial procedure must be followed.

According to De Smet (1868-1927) [10] the impediment of clandestinity—as he calls it—does not appear among the excepted cases of canon 1990, although it did appear among the excepted cases of the decree of the year 1889, and hence, if one keeps in mind that the enumeration of impediments in canon 1990 is exhaustive, one cannot count clandestinity among the excepted cases. Outside of the case, therefore, in which the juridical form had been neglected completely to such an extent that even the appearance of a marriage is lacking, he holds that the judicial process must be followed, even in cases in which the substantial defect of the form can be proved from certified and authentic documents. However, De Smet continues, there are some authors who follow a milder interpretation and state that the appeal to the court of second instance by the defender of the bond may be omitted, or that the case can be placed on the same basis with cases in which the form has been neglected completely.

Payen [11] asks: What about cases of nullity by reason of defect of form? And he answers that, when the marriage is certainly null because the substantial form has been neglected completely, so that

[10] *De Matrimonio*, n. 702bis.

[11] *De Matrimonio*, III, 572, n. 2721.

even the external appearance of a true marriage is lacking, a true process is not required, but it is sufficient to make an investigation into the free status of the parties. If the case occurs, it can be settled by the ordinary, or the pastor after the latter has consulted the ordinary on the case. The same procedure can be followed if one of the spouses clearly stated before the witnesses: "I do not," in answer to the question proposed by the priest, because in this case the marriage lacks the appearance of a true marriage. But a judicial process seems to be required if one of the spouses, when questioned during the marriage ceremony, remains silent, but goes through with the ceremony itself.

What about a case of nullity, Payen continues, when the juridical form is vitiated by a material defect? It is true that the form has been observed by the parties, but there exists a substantial defect in the form. Now it may be asked whether a case in which the form has been neglected completely is the same as a case in which the form is invalidated by reason of a substantial defect. In a case of this kind a distinction must be made between that which is evident and certain and that which is less evident and less certain. Therefore, there can be two cases, one in which the defect is evident and manifest, and the other in which the defect is obscure and hidden.

1°. The defect is not evident.—If the defect in the form, *e. g.*, that the priest did not receive a proper authorization, is not manifest or evident, then the case cannot be the same as the case in which the parties failed to observe the form completely. Inasmuch as the juridical form has been observed, but the substantial defect is evident, the marriage has at least the external appearance or semblance of a true marriage. Therefore a strictly judicial process is required and an appeal to the tribunal of the second instance is necessary.

2°. The defect is clearly manifest.—If the defect of the form, *e. g.*, that the pastor was not present, or that only one witness was present, is manifest and clear, it is disputed among authors whether the case in which the form was substantially invalidated is to be handled in the same manner as the case in which the form was neglected completely.

a. According to some, the longer and more difficult part of the judicial process can be omitted, namely, the proofs, for according to the norms of canon 1747 notorious facts do not need to be proved. Furthermore, Payen asks, is the defender of the marriage bond freed of the obligation of bringing the case to a new hearing in second instance? The author replies that the opinion which defends the option of the defender of the bond is very probable.

b. On the contrary, others state that, in the case of a very evident defect in regard to the form, it must be said that there is room for the above explained teaching which regards such a union as devoid of even the appearance of a true marriage. Correspondingly the norms of the answer of the Pontifical Commission, issued on October 16, 1919, n. 17, can be followed, or the prescriptions of canon 1990 can be applied. Payen concludes that, if the form has been neglected completely, the ordinary can settle the case by declaring the marriage null, but that if there is the appearance of a true marriage, the ordinary can follow the prescriptions of canon 1990, for the canon extends rather than restricts the decree of the Holy Office of 1889.

According to Prümmer (1866-1931),[12] the ordinary can, without having to follow any judicial process, and apart from the intervention of the defender of the bond, declare null and void any marriage which was entered into without the necessary assistance of the pastor. From this statement one may negatively infer that a judicial process is necessary whenever the marriage took place in the presence of a priest, but is rendered invalid because of a substantial defect in the form itself.

Gasparri (1852-1934),[13] stresses the fact that the defect of form, formerly known as the impediment of clandestinity, is not mentioned in canon 1990. He also regards the list of impediments as recounted in that canon to be exhaustive, that is, all-inclusive. Consequently he contends that a marriage in the contraction of which the form was indeed observed, but became vitiated by a substantial defect, can be declared null "in a summary manner." He bases this statement on the doctrine of canon 1747, n. 1, according to which notorious and evident facts no longer require proof regarding their existence. With the phrase, "in a summary manner," Gasparri refers not to

[12] *Manuale Iuris Canonici*, p. 629, n. 544.

[13] *De Matrimonio*, n. 1283.

the summary process delineated in canon 1990, but rather implies that the ordinary judicial procedure must still be followed. The investigation will proceed "in a summary manner" precisely because the facts in the case are evident and notorious, and therefore do not call for the usual extended procedure requisite for the gathering of convincing evidence and conclusive proof.

Wernz-Vidal (1842-1914) (1867-1938),[14] state that clandestinity or defect of form is numbered among the excepted cases in the decree of the Holy Office of 1889, but is not mentioned in canon 1990. Inasmuch as the list of cases enumerated in canon 1990 is exhaustive, a case of nullity arising from a lack of the requisite form cannot be numbered among these cases, for the omission is one of set purpose and design. After the promulgation of the Code of Canon Law, it is quite obvious from a response of the Pontifical Commission on October 16, 1919, that a judicial process is not required when the form of marriage has been neglected completely by the parties, *e. g.*, when the parties contracted a mere civil marriage, but that it is sufficient that an investigation be made concerning the free status of the parties, such as is required before parties contract a marriage. If it is determined that the parties completely neglected to observe the form, the case can be settled by the ordinary, or by the pastor after the latter has consulted the ordinary. However, a case in which the form of marriage has been neglected completely is not the same as a case in which the form has indeed been observed but the marriage has become invalidated by reason of a substantial defect in the form. In many cases the substantial defect in the form is quite evident and notorious, *e. g.*, the pastor has assisted at a marriage outside of his territory without due authorization, or a priest has assisted at a marriage without any authorization. But while these cases are quite evident, it is very rare that certified and authentic documents can be obtained. It seems, then, that these cases are provided for sufficiently in the general norms of the judicial process, for according to canon 1747 notorious facts do not need proof, and therefore the longer and more difficult part of a judicial process can be foregone almost completely. Since canon 1749 places the obligation on the judge not to admit the presentation of proofs which seem to be asked

[14] *Ius Canonicum*, V, *Ius Matrimoniale*, n. 705.

for the sake of delaying the conclusion of the trial, the judge *ex officio* must expedite these cases in order to prevent the emergence of harm for the parties. Even though the defender of the marriage bond is free to appeal the case, Wernz-Vidal believe that it can be held with solid probability that in his strict line of duty the defender of the bond is excused from appealing the case. If the defender, then, has not appealed the case, the ordinary of the first instance can declare that the parties are free to contract a new marriage.

In the light of the divers opinions here recounted, one may propose the following conclusions:

a. It is evident that the case of a complete lack of form is not the same as the case in which the form has indeed been observed, but becomes vitiated because of some substantial defect. Therefore the administrative procedure cannot be employed if there is the appearance of a true marriage, even though the marriage be invalid by reason of a substantial defect in the form. This is in accordance with article 231 of the Instruction, in which a clear distinction is made in paragraphs 1 and 2.

b. If there is the appearance of a true marriage, but there exists a substantial defect in the form, the summary process as outlined in canon 1990 cannot be followed, for it is generally admitted that the list of cases enumerated in canon 1990 is exhaustive, and that only those cases which are mentioned in canon 1990 may be tried by means of the summary process outlined in that canon. This is also evident from the letter of the Apostolic Delegate to the United States, in which letter the Apostolic Delegate does not give his own personal opinion, but expresses the mind of the Holy See on the subject.

c. All cases in which the juridical form has been observed must be tried according to the norms of the ordinary and solemn process. This is evident from the wording of the second paragraph of Article 231 of the Instruction, which states that in a case of doubt the question must be settled in accordance with the rules of the ordinary process. However, if the case is so evident that there is no likelihood for the opposite to be true, then a lengthy procedure for the gathering of proof is not required as long as the fact is notorious, for according to canon 1747, n. 1, notorious facts do not need to be proved.

This shortens the whole trial considerably, and thus as far as the duration of the procedure is concerned, it scarcely if at all exceeds the time requisite for the summary process as outlined in canons 1990 and following. The defender of the marriage bond has the obligation to appeal the case under these circumstances, for this obligation falls within the scope of his office. If the case is not obvious and clear, then the ordinary process must be employed, and the proofs must be gathered according to the norms of the canons. If under these circumstances the marriage is declared null, the defender of the bond must appeal the case to the tribunal of the second instance in accordance with the duties of his office.

d. The ordinary process must be followed in cases in which it is doubted whether the parties were bound to observe the canonical form of marriage, or in cases in which it is doubted whether the marriage was contracted before a priest or a civil official or a non-Catholic minister, for these are the conditions enumerated in § 1, of Article 231. If there exists a doubt about any of these conditions the ordinary process must be followed.

1. Recourse and Appeal

Voluntary jurisdiction is exercised whenever the strict formalities of a judicial process are not required in the law. Hence, whatever jurisdiction is exercised in an administrative process must be classified as voluntary jurisdiction. The act issued in virtue of this power is called a decree. Legal redress against such a decree is usually called recourse. Hence the terms *recourse* and *decree* ordinarily relate to a procedure in which there has been an exercise of voluntary jurisdiction.[15]

[15] Can. 1868, 2: "Ceterae iudicis pronuntiationes *decreta* vocantur." Cf. also S. R. R., *Quaestio incidentalis,* 23 apr. 1923, *coram R. P. D. Francisco Parrillo,* dec. IX, n. 4: "Ea quae tanquam iudices Episcopi gerunt, tribunalibus ordine hierarchico superioribus plene subiiciuntur; sed ea quae agunt tanquam administratores aut disciplinae moderatores, nullos habent iudices, nisi SS. Congregationes; unde a decretis administrativo vel disciplinari tramite latis 'non datur appellatio seu recursus ad Rotam, sed de huiusmodi recursibus *exclusive* cognoscunt SS. Congregationes.'"—*S. R. R. Dec.,* XV (1923), 85. Cf. also S. R. R. *Competentiae,* 27 apr. 1928, *coram R. P. D. Josepho Florczak,*

A recourse is a complaint to a superior because the party believes himself to be wronged or dealt with inequitably by the decree. Therefore if a party feels that an injustice or an inequity has been committed against him, he may seek recourse against the decree that was issued by the competent ecclesiastical authority in a case of defect of the proper canonical form. If the decree was issued by the vicar general or anyone delegated by the local ordinary, or by the pastor or anyone delegated by him, the party may seek the recourse with the bishop of the diocese; and if the decree was issued by the bishop of the diocese, the party may seek recourse with the Holy See. The Metropolitan cannot accept the recourse of the party, because the Metropolitan as such has no jurisdiction over the party. It is only in strictly judicial matters that the Metropolitan tribunal constitutes the court of appeal.[16] If the redress which is sought existed in the nature of an appeal, then the appeal would be placed with the court of second instance; but inasmuch as the redress remains in the nature of a recourse, the superior to the bishop is the Roman Pontiff.

A recourse may have either a non-suspensive or a suspensive effect. A recourse is non-suspensive in its effect when the decree remains in force and must be obeyed while the recourse is pending; It is suspensive in its effect when the act of the superior is regarded as non-existent and cannot be executed until the decision of the higher authority conforms to it.[17] Inasmuch as the decree issued by the local ordinary or the pastor in cases of defect of form affects the status of the person or persons, the execution of the decree will be suspended if the party has sought recourse with the higher authority. The parties, therefore, could not be forced to separate, if the competent ecclesiastical authority declares the marriage null by reason of defect of form, provided that the parties have recourse to the su-

dec. XIV, n. 7: "Dicitur *appellatio,* et non *recursus,* ut in casu reiectionis libelli (can. 1709, § 3), agnoscendo videlicet declarationi incompetentiae, sive detur in forma decreti ante initium iudicii, sive in forma sententiae interlocutoriae ob motam exceptionem aut ex officio ad normam can. 1611, *vim sententiae definitivae.*"—*S. R. R. Dec.,* XX (1928), 138.

[16] Cf. can. 1594.

[17] Eichmann, *Prozessrecht,* p. 178.

perior; nor could the parties be forced to resume cohabitation, if the competent authority decrees that the marriage is valid. The jurisdiction of the local ordinary or the pastor, if the latter handled the case, remains suspended in its effective exercise until the higher authority has rendered a concordant decision. In the making of this recourse all the documents that have been submitted in the case must be forwarded to the higher superior. It seems that in the cases of defect of form the Holy See, instead of settling the matter, will instruct the ordinary to institute a regular judicial process, and then to render a sentence against which the parties can appeal.

The recourse must be interposed with the higher superior within a reasonable time after the issuing of the decree, and it seems that a period of ten days would be a reasonable time.[18] The interval during which recourse is available must be considered as a *tempus utile* and not as a *tempus continuum*. The notion of *tempus utile* or available time has slightly changed with the years. The concept as it exists today is that time is said to be *utile* if it does not lapse when one could not actually use it. If ten days of *tempus utile*, for instance, are given for an appeal, and the person in question is hindered from so doing two days, these two days are not counted and two extra days are added, but this is done only once it becomes clear that a legal impediment really prevented the person from appealing.[19]

There is no reference to the time-period during which recourse may or must be made to the Holy See in cases of declaration of nullity of a marriage. In some cases similar to the declaration of nullity the Holy See decreed that the recourse mentioned had to be made within ten days of *tempus utile*.[20]

[18] Cf. can. 1881.

[19] Dubé, *The General Principles for the Reckoning of Time in Canon Law*, The Catholic University of America Canon Law Studies, n. 144 (Washington. D. C.: The Catholic University of America Press, 1941), p. 67.

[20] S. C. Conc. *Resolutio*, 14 ian. 1924: "Quale temporis spatium concedatur ad recursum interponendum a definitivo decreto remotionis, ad effectum canonis 2146, § 3, C. I. C. in casu." "R.—Tempus utile ad recursum interponendum a definitivo decreto remotionis, ad effectum § 3 canonis 2146 Codicis, esse decendium ab intimatione eiusdem decreti, supputandum ad normam canonis 34, § 3, n. 3, et canonis 35, certiore facto Ordinario loci ab ipso recurrente de legitime interposito recursu ad Apostolicam Sedem."—*AAS*, XVI (1924), 162.

If the parties in the case are both Catholics, the case must be sent to the S. Congregation of the Sacraments;[21] but if a non-Catholic is involved in the case, the Holy Office is exclusively competent.[22]

Strictly judicial jurisdiction is that which is exercised with the exact observance of all the formalities of legal procedure. The act of disposal resulting therefrom is set forth in a sentence. This sentence may be either interlocutory or definitive. An interlocutory sentence settles an incidental case, whereas the definitive sentence decides the principal issue.[23] Legal redress against such a sentence is called an appeal.[24] The appeal is a complaint brought from an inferior judge, who pronounced a sentence, to a higher judge, inasmuch as the party against whom the sentence was given believes himself wronged or his rights encroached upon by the former sentence.[25]

Appeal and sentence are usually correlative terms and connote the last stages in the fulfillment of the judicial formalities in a case. In defect of form cases, therefore, an appeal may be made if the case has gone through the judicial formalities of a trial. Whenever the judicial formalities are required according to paragraph 2 of Article 231 of the Instruction, an appeal may be made by either the parties, who believe themselves wronged by the former sentence, or by the promoter of justice if he took part in the case, or by the defender of the bond if the promoter of justice and the defender of the bond in accord with the rules of law feel that the public welfare has been injured.[26]

2. Expenses

A few words may be added here in regard to the expenses incurred, and in regard to what the people should be asked to render for the service connected with the granting of the decree of nullity. It is

[21] Cf. can. 249.

[22] Cf. can. 247.

[23] Cf. cans. 1840, § 2; 1868, § 1.

[24] Cf. can. 1879.

[25] Augustine, *A Commentary on Canon Law,* VII, 318; Doheny, *Canonical Procedure in Matrimonial Cases,* p. 142; Coronata, *Institutiones Iuris Canonici,* n. 1408.

[26] Augustine, *op. cit.,* VII, 318; cf. also Art. 212 ss.

quite obvious that expenses are connected with the issuing of a declaration of nullity. The printing of forms, the correspondence, etc., are expenses that should be taken care of in due proportion by the parties who petition the decree of nullity. If the marriage is declared null through an administrative procedure, it seems that a fee of $15.00 would not be too much to ask of the parties. This fee, however, in order that it may exist as a uniform fee throughout the province, should be determined by the bishops of the province either on the occasion of a provincial council, or at the time of the bishops' regional meeting, namely, when they meet to discuss the different affairs of the province.[27] If the parties are unable to pay the stipulated amount, they should give at least what they are equitably able to give. If the parties are poor, and cannot give anything, they should be excused from any and every obligation in the matter.

A fee of at least $25.00 should be considered payable if an ordinary process must be followed, but if simultaneously the facts are so evident that no proof is required. This fee should also be a set fee for the whole province, and should be determined at either the provincial council or the bishops' meeting.[28] If the facts which surround the case which is under investigation are somewhat obscure and dubious, so that the proofs must be gathered in the laborious way that a full judicial trial quite normally demands, then the parties should pay that amount which has already been established as the acknowledged fee in the different provinces throughout the country.

On July 1, 1932, the S. Congregation of the Sacraments issued a letter addressed to Archbishops, bishops, and local ordinaries requesting them to submit to Rome a complete annual report of the work of their respective tribunals.[29] To facilitate the work of tribunals and to establish a uniform system for all the ecclesiastical courts in the world, the S. Congregation of the Sacraments has seen fit to publish special forms for the use of the tribunals. These forms are three in number. It is clear from the arrangement of the forms that

[27] Cf. cans. 292 and 1507.

[28] Cf. can. 1909, § 1.

[29] Cf. *AAS,* XXIV (1932), 272.

they are to be used exclusively for the following cases: 1. Formal cases dealing with the nullity of marriage; 2. Informal or summary cases tried according to the provisions of canon 1990. The second part of Form III is intended for a schematic report of all the cases on the entire roster of the tribunal for a given year. Mention should be made of the cases decided because of lack of form.

CONCLUSIONS

1.—Before the Council of Trent no procedure existed for the declaration of nullity of marriages contracted outside the Church.

2.—After the Council of Trent it was the constant practice of the Church to declare marriages null through an administrative process, if these marriages were evidently null by reason of complete lack of form.

3.—The decree of nullity can be granted at the request of Catholics, baptized non-Catholics and even infidels.

4.—The term *ordinary* in connection with the declaration of nullity embraces all persons included within the classification mentioned in canon 198, 2. The term *pastor* embraces also all parochial vicars with the exception of the parochial assistant.

5.—The number of documents must be sufficient to beget moral certainty before a declaration of nullity can be granted.

6.—A search in the files of the chancery offices of other dioceses is not necessary to determine whether a simple convalidation or sanation has been granted in a particular case.

7.—Whenever the form of marriage has been observed but is vitiated through a substantial defect the ordinary rules of procedure must be followed to settle the question of validity or nullity of the marriage.

APPENDIX

FORM 1

Letter to be sent to parish of baptism of the Catholic party by priest presenting the case.

PARISH OF N. N.

________________ vs. ________________

Date:

Reverend dear Father:

Will you kindly return this form to me as soon as possible, bearing an exact transcript of the BAPTISMAL RECORD of ________________
child of ________________ and ________________
who was baptized in your church on (or about) ________________

Please make all the notations indicated below (Can. 470, § 3). This record is necessary in the investigation of the marriage case designated above.

While thanking you for your kindness, may I assure you of my readiness to reciprocate the favor at any time.

Sincerely yours,

(Rev.) ________________

Address ________________

Please do not detach.

BAPTISMAL RECORD

Name ________________

Parents: Father ________________ Religion ________________
Mother ________________ Religion ________________

Date of Birth ________________

Date of Baptism ________________ Minister ________________

Parish of Baptism ________________
Name of Parish *City or Town*

Sponsors ________________

The following notations are found in this record:

Baptism (absolute, conditional, convert) ________________
Confirmation (Cans. 470, §2; 798) ________________
Marriage (Cans. 470, § 2; 1103, § 2) ________________

Signed ________________
(Pastor-Assistant)

Date:

Parish Seal. Place:

FORM 2

Letter to be sent to parish of confirmation of the Catholic party, if the party was confirmed in a different parish than the parish of baptism, or if the baptismal record does not note the fact of confirmation. This letter is absolutely necessary, if the Catholic party is the child of non-Catholic parents or of a mixed marriage.

PARISH OF N. N.

______________ vs. ______________

Date:

Reverend dear Father:

Will you kindly return this form to me as soon as possible, bearing an exact transcript of the CONFIRMATION RECORD of ______________ child of ______________ and ______________, who was confirmed in your church on (or about) ______________

This record is necessary in the investigation of the marriage case designated above.

While thanking you for your kindness, may I assure you of my readiness to reciprocate the favor at any time.

Sincerely yours,

(Rev.) ______________

Address ______________

Please do not detach.

CONFIRMATION RECORD

Name ______________

Parents: Father ______________ Religion ______________
Mother ______________ Religion ______________

Date of Birth ______________

Date of Baptism ______________

Date of Confirmation ______________ Minister ______________

Parish of Confirmation ______________
Name of Parish *City or Town*

Sponsor(s) ______________

Signed ______________
(*Pastor-Assistant*)

Date:

Parish Seal. Place:

FORM 3

Letter to be sent to parish of first Holy Communion of the Catholic party. This letter is necessary, if the party was born of non-Catholic parents or of a mixed marriage, and never received the sacrament of confirmation.

PARISH OF N. N.

________________ vs. ________________

Date:

Reverend dear Father:

Will you kindly return this form to me as soon as possible, bearing an exact transcript of the RECORD OF FIRST HOLY COMMUNION of ________________ child of ________________ and ________________, who received First Holy Communion in your church on (or about) ________________

This record is necessary in the investigation of the marriage case designated above.

While thanking you for your kindness, may I assure you of my readiness to reciprocate the favor at any time.

Sincerely yours,

(Rev.) ________________

Address ________________

Please do not detach.

RECORD OF FIRST HOLY COMMUNION

This is to certify that ________________
child of ________________ and ________________
who was baptized on ________________
received First Holy Communion in this church on ________________

Signed ________________

(*Pastor-Assistant*)

Name of Church:
Place:

Date:
Parish Seal.

FORM 4

Letter to be sent to priest of parish where the Catholic party attended either the parochial or public school and received Catechism instruction. This letter is necessary to ascertain if the party received a Catholic education in the absence of records of Confirmation or first Holy Communion.

PARISH OF N. N.

____________________ vs. ____________________

Date:

Reverend dear Father:

Will you kindly return the attached form to me as soon as possible, stating exactly what Catholic education ____________________ ____________ child of ____________ and ____________ ____________ received.

This record is necessary in the investigation of the marriage case designated above.

While thanking you for your kindness, may I assure you of my readiness to reciprocate the favor at any time.

Sincerely yours,

(Rev.) ____________________

Address ____________________

Please do not detach.

SCHOOL RECORD

This is to certify that ____________________ child of ____________ and ____________ attended ____________________

(Parochial school—Public school)

from the year ____________ to the year ____________, and received the proper instruction in Christian doctrine.

Signed ____________________

(*Pastor-Assistant*)

Name of Church:

Place:
Date:

Parish Seal.

FORM 5

The Supplementary Oath

The party having been instructed concerning the sanctity of an oath and being fully aware of the possible consequences of perjury, takes the following oath:

I, ____________________________, hereby solemnly

swear that my marriage contracted before ____________________
(Civil official—

____________________ on ____________________
Protestant minister)

with ____________________________, was never rectified by the Church.

Signed ____________________

Subscribed and sworn to before me this ______________ day of

____________________, 19____, at ____________________
(City, State)

____
(Signature and seal of pastor, or notary.)

FORM 6

Affidavit of a Trustworthy Catholic

The person having acknowledged that he (she) fully understands the nature and sanctity of an oath, and having been duly sworn, answers the following questions:

1. What is your name?
2. What is your age?
3. What is your religion?
4. Can you identify yourself?
5. Were you ever baptized?
6. If so, where?
7. When were you baptized?
8. Did you make your first Holy Communion?
9. If so, when and where?
10. Are you a practical Catholic at the present time?
11. To what parish do you belong?
12. What is your present address?
13. Do you know the party in the case?
14. Are you a relative?
15. Was he (she) ever married?
16. If so, to whom?
17. When was he (she) married?
18. Where was he (she) married?
19. By whom was he (she) married?
20. Was this marriage ever rectified by the Church?
21. What opportunity have you had for knowing this?
22. Was .... ever baptized?
23. If so, when and where?
24. What opportunity have you had for knowing this?
25. Was his (her) mother a Catholic at the time of his (her) birth?
26. If not, what was the mother's religious status at that time?
27. Was his (her) father a Catholic at the time of his (her) birth?
28. If not, what was the father's religious status at that time?
29. Did he (she) ever receive First Communion?
30. If so, when, where, and at what age?
31. Was he (she) ever confirmed?
32. If so, when and where and at what age?
33. Did .... ever attend Mass on Sundays?
34. If so, for how long a time and how frequently?
35. Can you state whether .... knew the doctrines of the Catholic Faith?
36. Was .... ever instructed in the Catholic Religion?
37. If so, to what extent?
38. At the time of his (her) marriage to .... did he (she) have a fair knowledge of the Catholic Religion?

After giving the above testimony and having read it, I verify the same and hereunto subscribe my name.

Signed ....

Sworn and subscribed to in my presence this .... day of ...., 19......, at ....

Signed ....

Seal. (Pastor or notary)

FORM 7

Petition for declaration of nullity because of defect of the proper canonical form.

His Excellency,
The Most Reverend N. N.
Bishop of N. N.
Your Excellency:

I, ______________________
a baptized Catholic
an apostate
a baptized non-Catholic
an unbaptized non-Catholic

neglecting the canonical form of marriage prescribed by canon 1094 of the Code of Canon Law, having obtained a civil license in the

(County, City) of ______________________
in the State of ______________________, attempted

marriage with ______________________
a baptized Catholic
an apostate
a baptized non-Catholic
an unbaptized non-Catholic

on ______________________, 19____, in the
City of ______________________, State of ______________________,
before ______________________. I have
(Civil official—non-Catholic minister)
obtained a civil divorce in the (County, City) of ______________________,
in the State of ______________________, on ______________________, 19____,
on the ground of ______________________.

I claim this attempted marriage to be null and void because of defect of the proper canonical form, and I humbly petition that it be so declared by legitimate ecclesiastical authority.

In proof of my claim, I herewith submit the following:

Yours sincerely in Christ,

____
Petitioner

Date:
Place:

Signed ______________________________
(Pastor-Assistant)

Fee enclosed for Chancery expenses $____________

QUESTIONNAIRE

I, ______________________________ being duly admonished of the nature and gravity of an oath, and being duly sworn, and having identified himself (herself) by means of ______________________________
(Passport, Driver's License, etc.)
answer the following questions:

1. (a) What is your full name?
   (b) What is your maiden name (or alias)?
2. What is your address:
3. What is your occupation?
4. What is your religion?
5. (a) When were you born?
   (b) Where were you born?
6. (a) When were you baptized?
   (b) Where were you baptized?
7. (a) What is your father's name?
   (b) What was his religion at the time of your birth?
8. (a) What was your mother's maiden name?
   (b) What was her religion at the time of your birth?
9. (a) Did you attend a parochial school?
   (b) Give name of schools, years of attendance and corresponding dates?
10. (a) Did you attend Catechism classes on Sundays?
    (b) Give name of parishes, years of attendance and corresponding dates.
11. (a) Did you receive the sacrament of first Holy Communion?
    (b) When and where did you receive this sacrament?
12. (a) Have you received the sacrament of confirmation?
    (b) When were you confirmed?
    (c) Where were you confirmed?
13. (a) How many times in your entire life have you entered or attempted marriage?
    (b) If you now desire to revalidate this marriage (or one of these marriages), give name of the consort of this union.
14. Regarding this ______________ (number of the contracted marriage) union, which you wish to have authoritatively declared null, state:
    (a) Name of (person you married) the consort at the time this union was contracted.

(b) Present name and address of that person.
(c) Date of marriage.
(d) Place of marriage.
(e) Where did you obtain the license for the marriage?
(f) Before what official did you contract or attempt the marriage?
(g) What religion was professed by the person you married?
(h) Was this union the first, second, ———— marriage of that person?
(i) State particulars of the previous marriage (marriages) on that person's part.

15. (a) Did you desire to marry that person in the presence of a Catholic priest?
(b) Did you request that person to marry you in the presence of a Catholic priest?
(c) If so, what was the result of that request?

16. Describe for what reason you were not married by a Catholic priest.

17. (a) How long did you live with that person?
(b) Where did you live with that person?

18. During the period of cohabitation with this spouse:
(a) Did you attend Mass on Sundays and Holydays?
(b) Did you attempt to frequent the sacraments of confession and Holy Communion?

19. (a) Did you ever speak to a Catholic priest to arrange for the convalidation of this marriage?
(b) If so, give results.

20. (a) Did you ever request a Catholic priest to obtain for you a *sanatio in radice* regarding this marriage?
(b) If so, give results.

21. Do you solemnly swear that this marriage was never rectified in the Catholic Church?

22. (a) Were any children born of this marriage?
(b) If so, give their names, birthdays, religion and particulars regarding their Catholic baptism.

23. (a) Has this marriage been dissolved by a civil divorce or annulment?
(b) If so, when, where and upon what grounds was the divorce granted?
(c) Who was the plaintiff?

24. Do you desire to contract marriage in the Catholic Church at the present time?
If so, (a) Name the person whom you wish to marry.
What is this person's address?
(b) What is the religion of this person?
(c) Is this person free to marry you?

25. (a) Have you already attempted marriage with this person outside the Church?
(b) When, where and before what official did you attempt this marriage?

26. (a) When do you propose to contract in the church the marriage you now have in prospect?
    (b) Where is its celebration to take place?
27. Do you desire to add anything to your testimony?

Here the testimony will be read to the deponent or by the deponent himself.

28. Do you desire to suppress or add anything in the above testimony?

Having given the above testimony in the presence of the hereinafter designated witness on the date specified, and having had the opportunity of examining all my answers, I do hereby solemnly swear that this my deposition is in accordance with the truth. So help me God and these His Holy Gospels.

Signed ....
Deponent.

Given at ....
Number *Street* *City* *State*

this the .... day of ...., 19........

....
Priest—Notary

Seal.

FORM 8

Letter to be sent to the Diocesan Curia by the priest who presents the case.

PARISH OF N. N.

His Excellency,
The Most Reverend N. N.
Bishop of N. N.

Your Excellency:

I am submitting to Your Excellency the case of

_______________ vs. _______________

_______________, the petitioner, claims that the marriage is null and void because of defect of the proper canonical form, and he (she) humbly petitions that it be so declared by legitimate ecclesiastical authority.

I am enclosing the following documents:

Yours sincerely in Christ,

____
Pastor.

Date:
Place:

Parish Seal.

FORM 9

DECREE OF NULLITY

DIOCESE OF N. N.

No.

________________ vs. ________________

DECRETUM

Cum ex certis et authenticis documentis Nobis evidenter constet matrimonium inter D ________________ et D ________________, qu____ ad formam canonicam celebrationis matrimonii (cans. 1094 and 1099) observandam certo tenebatur, die ________________, mensis ________________, 19____, attentatum, OB DEFECTUM FORMAE CANONICAE nullum fuisse ab initio, Nos, infrascriptus Ordinarius dioecesis ________________, iuxta normas Instructionis a S. Cong. de disciplina Sacramentorum, die 15 Aug. 1936, art. 231, traditae, praefatum matrimonium nullum irritumque coram Deo et Ecclesia declaramus.

____

Episcopus Dioecesis N. N.

Datum ex Aedibus Curiae Episcopalis, N. N.

die ________________, mensis ________________, 19____.

____

Notarius.

FORM 10

Letter to be sent to priest when the decree of nullity has been granted.

DIOCESE OF N. N.

No.

__________________ vs. __________________

Dear Father:

His Excellency, the Most Reverend Bishop has instructed me to transmit to you the enclosed decree of nullity of the above mentioned marriage. The legal papers which were submitted in the case are herewith transmitted to you with the direction that they be returned to the party concerned.

To avoid any doubt in the future about the validity of the marriage which the petitioner now wishes to enter, proper annotation should be made of this decree in the marriage register. In accordance with canon 1103, § 2, notice of this marriage is to be sent to the parish where the petitioner was baptized.

This decree is not to be given to the petitioner, but is to be kept in the parish archives. However, the petitioner may be given a copy of it.

The petitioner should be properly instructed that this decree is accorded no civil effect whatsoever.

Yours sincerely in Christ,

____

Chancellor.

Place:
Date:

FORM 11

Letter of priest to the place of baptism of the Catholic party or parties after the sentence of nullity has been granted.

PARISH OF N. N.

________________ vs. ________________

NAME OF BAPTIZED:
PARISH OF BAPTISM:
DATE OF BAPTISM:

Reverend dear Father:

The person designated above, who was baptized in your church, contracted a marriage which was subsequently alleged to be null and void because of the failure to observe the canonical form as prescribed by canons 1094 and 1099 of the Code of Canon Law.

The allegation of nullity was sustained as the result of a canonical trial conducted by the Tribunal of the Diocese of N. N., and a sentence of nullity was accordingly granted on ________________

Will you kindly make an annotation of this sentence in the baptismal register?

Thanking you for your kindness, I am,

____
Pastor.

Date:
Place:

FORM 12

CHANCERY OFFICE MEMORANDUM

____________________ vs. ____________________

Attempted marriage was contracted on ____________________

before ______________________________________

(Civil Official—Protestant Minister)

Decree of nullity was granted on ____________________

by ____________________

The following documents were submitted in the case:

____

Chancellor.

BIBLIOGRAPHY

Sources

Acta Apostolicae Sedis, Commentarium Officiale, Romae, 1909—

Acta et Decreta Concilii Plenarii Baltimorensis Tertii, Baltimorae, 1886.

Acta Sanctae Sedis, 41 vols., Romae, 1865-1908.

Bouscaren, T. L., *The Canon Law Digest,* 2 vols. and 1938 and 1941 Supplements, Milwaukee: The Bruce Publishing Company, 1934-1941.

Bullarium SSmi. Domini nostri Benedicti XIV, 4. ed., 4 vols., Venetiis, 1878.

Bruns, *Canones Apostolorum et Conciliorum saec. IV-VII,* 1 vol. in 2, 8°, Berolini, 1839.

Canones et Decreta Sacrosancti Oecumenici Concilii Tridentini sub Paulo III, Iulio III, et Pio IV Pontificibus Maximis, editio stereotypa, Ratisbonae, 1903.

Codex Iuris Canonici Pii X Pontificis Maximi iussu digestus Benedicti Papae XV auctoritate promulgatus, Romae: Typis Polyglottis Vaticanis, 1917.

Codicis Iuris Canonici Fontes cura Emi. Petri Card. Gasparri Editi, 9 vols., Romae (postea Civitate Vaticana): Typis Polyglottis Vaticanis, 1923-39. (Vols. VII, VIII, IX ed. cura et studio Emi. Iustiniani Card. Serédi.)

Corpus Iuris Canonici, Editio Lipsiensis II post Aemilii Ludovici Richteri curas instruxit Aemilius Friedberg, 1879-1881. Editio anastatice repetita, Lipsiae: Tauchnitz, 1928.

Jaffé, Ph., *Regesta Pontificum Romanorum,* ed. secundam correctam et auctam auspiciis Guilelmi Wattenbach curaverunt F. Kaltenbrunner (ad annum 590), P. Ewald (anno 590-882), S. Löwenfeld (anno 882-1198), Lipsiae, 1885-1888.

Hartzheim, Joseph, *Concilia Germaniae,* 11 vols., Coloniae Augustae Agrippinensium, 1759-1790.

Mansi, Joannes, *Sacrorum Conciliorum Nova et Amplissima Collectio,* 53 vols. in 59, Parisiis, 1901-27.

Monumenta Germaniae Historica, 188 vols. incomplete, Hanoverae, 1826—

———, *Epistola,* 7 vols. in 4°, 1887-1928. T. VI, ed. E. Duemmler-E. Perels, Berolini: Apud Weidmannos, 1925.

Sacrae Romanae Rotae Decisiones seu Sententiae quae . . . prodierunt anno 1909—, Romae: Typis Vaticanis, 1912—

Schroeder, H. J., *Canons and Decrees of the Council of Trent,* St. Louis: B. Herder Book Company, 1941.

———, *Disciplinary Decrees of the General Councils,* St. Louis: B. Herder Book Company, 1937.

Thesaurus Resolutionum Sacrae Congregationis Concilii, 167 vols., Romae: 1718-1908.

Reference Works

Alford, C. B., *Jus Matrimoniale Comparatum,* New York: P. J. Kenedy & Sons, 1938.

Ayrinhac, H. A., *Marriage Legislation in the New Code of Canon Law,* New and revised edition by P. J. Lydon, New York, Boston, Cincinnati, Chicago, San Francisco: Benziger Brothers, Inc., 1941.

Attwater, Donald, *The Catholic Eastern Churches,* Revised Edition, Milwaukee: The Bruce Publishing Company, 1937.

[Bachofen], Charles Augustine, *A Commentary on Canon Law,* 8 vols., Vol. II, 6. ed., St. Louis-London: B. Herder Book Company, 1936.

Benedetti, Ivo, *Ordo Iudicialis Processus Canonici Super Nullitate Matrimonii Instruendi iuxta Instructionem a S. Congregatione de Sacramentis,* Novissima editio, Taurini: Marietti, 1938.

Bridges, J., *History of Northamptonshire,* Oxford, 1791.

Cappello, Felix M., *Summa Iuris Canonici,* 3 vols., Vols. I and II, 3. ed., Romae: Apud Aedes Universitatis Gregorianae, 1938-1939.

———, *Tractatus Canonico-Moralis de Sacramentis,* 3 vols. in 6, Vol. III, 3. ed., *De Matrimonio,* Taurinorum Augustae: Officina Libraria Marietti, 1939.

Carberry, J. J., *The Juridical Form of Marriage,* The Catholic University of America Canon Law Studies, n. 84, Washington, D. C.: The Catholic University of America, 1934.

Chelodi, J., *Ius Matrimoniale iuxta Codicem Iuris Canonici,* 4. ed., recognita et aucta a Vigilio Dalpiaz, Tridenti: Libreria Moderna Editrice A. Ardesi, 1937.

Coronata, Matthaeus Conte a, *Institutiones Iuris Canonici,* 5 vols., Taurini: Marietti, 1933-1939; Vols. I-II, 2. ed., 1939; Vol. III, 1933; Vol. IV, 1935; Vol. V, 1936.

De Meester, A., *Juris Canonici et Juris Canonico-Civilis Compendium,* nova ed., 3 vols. in 4, Brugis: Desclée, De Brouwer, 1921-1928.

De Smet, M., *Tractatus Theologico-Canonicus de Sponsalibus et Matrimonio,* 4. ed., Brugis: Car. Beyaert, 1927.

Doheny, William J., *Canonical Procedure in Matrimonial Cases,* Milwaukee: The Bruce Publishing Company, 1938.

———, *Practical Manual for Marriage Cases,* Milwaukee: The Bruce Publishing Company, 1938.

Dubé, A. J., *The General Principles for the Reckoning of Time in Canon Law,* The Catholic University of America Canon Law Studies, n. 144, Washington, D. C.: The Catholic University of America Press, 1941.

Eichmann, E., *Das Prozessrecht des Codex Iuris Canonici,* Paderborn, 1921.

———, *Lehrbuch des Kirchenrechts,* 4. ed., 2 vols., Paderborn, 1934.

Fanfani, L. I., *De Iure Parochorum,* ed. altera, Taurini: Marietti, 1936.

Feije, H. J., *De Impedimentis et Dispensationibus Matrimonialibus,* 3. ed., Lovanii: Typis Caroli Peeters, 1885.

Feltoe, C., *Sacramentarium Leonianum,* Cambridge, 1896.

Ferraris, Lucius, *Prompta Bibliotheca, Canonica, Iuridica, Moralis, Theologica, necnon Ascetica, Polemica, Rubristica, Historica,* 9 vols., Romae, 1885-1899.

Friedberg, E., *Das Recht* der *Eheschliessung in der geschichtlichen Entwicklung,* Leipzig, 1865.

Funk, Y., *Patres Apostolici,* 2. ed., 2 vols., Tubingae, 1901.

Gasparri, P., *Tractatus Canonicus de Matrimonio,* Editio nova ad mentem Codicis I. C., 2 vols., Romae: Typis Polyglottis Vaticanis, 1932.

Gerlach, H., *Lehrbuch des katholischen Kirchenrechts,* 3. ed., Paderborn, 1876.

Heck, P., *Der Eheverteidiger im kanonischen Eheprozess,* Bonn: Ludwig Röhrscheid Verlag, 1937.

Hefele, C., *Konziliengeschichte,* 2. ed., 9 vols., Vols. VIII and IX continued by Card. Hergenroether, Freiburg i. B., 1873-1890.

Heiner, F., *Katholisches Kirchenrecht,* 6. ed., 2 vols., Paderborn, 1913.

Hervé, J. M., *Manuale Theologiae Dogmaticae,* 13. ed., 4 vols., Parisiis: Apud Berche et Pagis, 1936.

Hilling, N., *Das Eherecht des Codex Iuris Canonici,* Freiburg i. B.: Josef Waibel, 1927.

———, *Das Personenrecht des Codex Iuris Canonici,* Paderborn: Ferdinand Schöningh, 1924.

Hofmann, Karl, *Die Freiwillige Gerichtsbarkeit im kanonischen Recht,* Paderborn: Ferdinand Schöningh, 1929.

Hohenlohe, E., *Das Prozessrecht des Codex Iuris Canonici,* Wien, 1921.

Hollnsteiner, J., *Die Sprachpraxis der S. Romana Rota in Ehenichtigkeitsprozessen seit Geltung des C. I. C.,* Freiburg i. B.: Herder, 1934.

Jone, H., *Gesetzbuch des kanonischen Rechtes,* 3 vols., Paderborn: Ferdinand Schöningh, 1939-1941.

Keene, M. J., *Religious Ordinaries and Canon 198,* The Catholic University of America Canon Law Studies, n. 135, Washington, D. C.: The Catholic University of America Press, 1942.

Knecht, A., *Handbuch des katholischen Eherechts,* Freiburg i. B.: Herder, 1928.

Koeniger, A. M., *Die Eheprozessordnung für die Diözesangerichte,* Kanonistische Studien und Texte, Bd. XI, Bonn: Ludwig Röhrscheid Verlag, 1937.

Köstler, Rudolf, *Das österreichische Konkordats-Eherecht,* Wien: Julius Springer, 1937.

Lega, M. Card., *Praelectiones De Iudiciis Ecclesiasticis,* 4 vols., Romae, 1896-1901; Vol. 1, 2. ed., Romae, 1905.

Lega, M.,-Bartocetti, V., *Commentarius in Iudicia Ecclesiastica iuxta Codicem Iuris Canonici,* 3 vols., Romae: Anonima Libraria Cattolica Italiana, 1938-1941.

Lietzmann, H., *Das Sacramentarium Gregorianum nach dem Aachener Urexemplar,* Münster i. W., Aschendorff'sche Verlagsbuchhandlung, 1921.

Lingen, Ch.-Reuss, P. A., *Causae selectae in S. C. Card. Concilii Trid. interpretum propositae per summaria precum ab anno 1823 usque ad annum 1869*, Ratisbonae, 1871.

Linneborn, J., *Grundriss des Eherechts nach dem Codex Iuris Canonici*, 4. und 5. Aufl., Paderborn: Ferdinand Schöningh, 1933.

Lombardi, Carolus, *Iuris Canonici Privati Institutiones*, 2. ed., 3 vols., Romae, 1901.

Lydon, P. J., *Ready Answers in Canon Law*, 2. ed., New York, Cincinnati, Chicago, San Francisco: Benziger Brothers, Inc., 1937.

Maroto, Philippus, *Institutiones Iuris Canonici ad normam Novi Codicis*, 2 vols., Vol. 1, 3. ed., Romae: apud Commentarium pro Religiosis, 1921.

May, G., *Marriage Laws and Decisions in the United States*, New York: Russell Sage Foundation, 1929.

Meier, C. A., *Penal Administrative Procedure Against Negligent Pastors*, The Catholic University of America Canon Law Studies, n. 140, Washington, D. C.: The Catholic University of America Press, 1941.

Migne, Jacques Paul, *Patrologiae Cursus Completus, Series Graeca*, 162 vols., Parisiis, 1857-1866.

———, *Patrologiae Cursus Completus, Series Latina*, 221 vols., Parisiis, 1844-1864.

Noldin, H.,-Schmitt, A., *Summa Theologiae Moralis*, 24. ed., 4 vols. in 3, Oeniponte: Typis et Sumptibus F. Rauch, 1936.

Noval, Joseph, *Commentarium Codicis Iuris Canonici*, Lib. IV, *De Processibus*, 2 vols., Romae: Marietti, 1920-1932.

Payen, G., *De Matrimonio in Missionibus ac potissimum in Sinis*, Tractatus Practicus et Casus, altera editio, 3 vols., Zi-ka-wei: In Typographia T'ou-se-we, 1936.

Petrovits, J. J., *The New Church Law on Matrimony*, 2. ed., Philadelphia: John Joseph McVey, 1926.

Pichler, Vitus, *Candidatus Iurisprudentiae Sacrae*, 4 vols., Ingolstadii, 1716.

Pirhing, E., *Ius Canonicum nova methodo explicatum*, 4 vols., Dilingae, 1676.

Portmann, H., *Wesen und Unauflöslichkeit der Ehe, Emsdetten*, Westfalen: Heinrich und J. Lechte, 1938.

Prince, J., *The Diocesan Chancellor*, The Catholic University of America Canon Law Studies, n. 167, Washington, D. C.: The Catholic University of America Press, 1942.

Prümmer, M., *Manuale Iuris Canonici*, 6. ed., quam curavit Engelbertus M. Münch, Friburgi Brisgoviae: Herder & Co., 1933.

Reiffenstuel, A., *Ius Canonicum Universum*, 7 vols., Venetiis, 1735.

Sägmüller, J. B., *Lehrbuch des katholischen Kirchenrechts*, 3. ed., 2 vols., Freiburg, 1914.

Schmalzgrueber, F., *Ius Ecclesiasticum Universum*, 12 vols., Romae, 1843-1845.

Schmier, F., *Iurisprudentia canonico-civilis*, 3 vols., Salisburgi, 1716.

Schönsteiner, Ferdinand, *Grundriss des kirchlichen Eherechts,* 2. ed., Wien: Verlag der Buchhandlung Ludwig Auer, 1937.

Silbernagl, I., *Lehrbuch des katholischen Kirchenrechts,* 3. ed., Regensburg, 1895.

Triebs, F., *Praktisches Handbuch des geltenden kanonischen Eherechts in Vergleichung mit dem deutschen staatlichen Eherecht,* Teil I-IV in einem Band, Gesamtausgabe, Breslau: Ostdeutsche Verlagsanstalt, 1933.

Vering, F. H., *Lehrbuch des katholischen, orientalischen und protestantischen Kirchenrechts,* 3. ed., Freiburg i. B., 1893.

Vermeersch, A., *Principia-Responsa-Consilia Theologiae Moralis,* 3. ed., 4 vols. in 3, Roma: Universita Gregoriana, 1933.

Vermeersch, A.,-Creusen, J., *Epitome Iuris Canonici,* 3 vols., Vol. I, 6. ed., 1937; Vol. II-III, 5. ed., Mechliniae-Romae: H. Dessain, 1934-1939.

Vromant, G., *Ius Missionariorum,* Vol. V, *De Matrimonio,* Louvain: Museum Lessianum, 1931.

Wanenmacher, Francis, *Canonical Evidence in Marriage Cases,* Philadelphia, Pa.: Dolphin Press, 1935.

Wenner, Joseph, *Die kirchliche Eheprozessordnung,* Textausgabe, Paderborn: Ferdinand Schöningh, 1937.

Wernz, F. X., *Ius Decretalium,* 6 vols., Romae, 1898-1905.

Wernz, F. X.,-Vidal, P., *Ius Canonicum,* 7 vols. in 8, Romae: Apud Aedes Universitatis Gregorianae, 1927-1938; tom. I, 1938; tom. II, 2. ed., 1928; tom. III, 1933; tom. IV, pars I, 1934; tom. IV, pars II, 1935; tom. V, 2. ed., 1928; tom. VI, 1927; tom. VII, 1937.

Willett, R. A., *The Probative Value of Documents in Ecclesiastical Trials,* The Catholic University of America Canon Law Studies, n. 171, Washington, D. C.: The Catholic University of America Press, 1942.

Wilson, H. A., *The Gelasian Sacramentary,* Oxford, 1894.

Woywod, S., *A Practical Commentary on the Code of Canon Law,* 5. ed., 2 vols., New York: Joseph F. Wagner, 1939.

Periodicals

Apollinaris, Romae, 1928—

Archiv für katholisches Kirchenrecht, Innsbruck, 1857-1861; Mainz, 1862—

Ephemerides Theologicae Lovanienses, Lovanii, 1924 —

Irish Ecclesiastical Record, Dublin, 1864—

Jurist, The, Washington, D. C., 1941—

Nouvelle Revue Théologique, Paris, 1869—

Periodica de Re Canonica et Morali utili Praesertim Religiosis et Missionariis, Bruges, 1905—

Theologische Quartalschrift, Tübingen, 1819—

Theologisch-praktische Quartalschrift, Linz, 1832—

Articles

Alford, C. B., "Common Law Marriages in Relation to the Code"—*The Jurist*, II (1942), 248-262.

De Smet, A., "Recentiores Variationes in re matrimoniali"—*Ephemerides Theologicae Lovaniensis*, I (1924), 558-579.

Freisen, J., "Die Entwicklung des kirchlichen Eheschliessungrechts"—*AKKR*, LIII (1885), 71-104.

Hannan, J. D., "Informal Marriages"—*The Jurist*, III (1943), 149-151.

Haring, J., "Das Klagerecht im kanonischen Eheprozess"—*AKKR*, CXV (1935), 111—

———, "Die Jurisdiktion des Pfarrvikars"—*Theol.-prakt. Quartalschrift*, LXXX (1922), 22-27.

———, "Eheungültigkeit wegen mangelnder Form"—*Theol.-prakt. Quartalschrift*, XCI (1938), 522-523.

———, "Fälle aus der Ehegerichtspraxis"—*Theol.-prakt. Quartalschrift*, LXXXIX (1936), 355-359.

Hilling, N., "Die Bedeutung der iurisdictio voluntaria und involuntaria im römischen Recht und im kanonischen Recht des Mittelalters und der Neuzeit"—*AKKR*, CV (1925), 449-473.

———, "Eine Entscheidung des hl. Offiziums über die kirchliche Gerichtsbarkeit zweier akatholischen Eheleute"—*AKKR*, CVII (1927), 569.

———, "Neueste Entscheidungen des Hl. Stuhles über das Ehehindernis der Religionsverschiedenheit, die Auflösung einer Naturehe und die Anwendung des Privilegium Paulinum"—*AKKR*, CVII (1927), 178-186.

Johnson, Jos., "De distinctione inter potestatem iudicialem et potestatem administrativam in iure canonico"—*Apollinaris*, IX (1936), 258-269.

Mocnik, V., "Das Klagerecht des *Promotor iustitiae* bei *vis et* metus"—*Theol.-prakt. Quartalschrift*, LXXXVII (1934), 145-149.

Mörsdorf, K., "Zur Eheprozessordnung für die Diözesangerichte vom 15 August 1936"—*Theologische Quartalschrift*, CXX (1939), 206-219.

Oesterle, P. G., "Ehe ohne Taufschein"—*Theol.-prakt. Quartalschrift*, XCIII (1940), 312-313.

———, "Wiederverehelichung einer geschiedenen Konvertitin"—*Theol.-prakt. Quartalschrift*, XC (1937), 679-680.

Rettenbacher, F., "Der Kooperator nach dem neuen Codex Iuris"—*Theol.-prakt. Quartalschrift*, LXXII (1919), 337-348.

Triebs, H., "Lose Blätter zum kanonischen Prozess"—*Theol.-prakt. Quartalschrift*, LXXXIX (1936), 485 und 691.

LIST OF ABBREVIATIONS

AAS—*Acta Apostolicae Sedis.*

AKKR—*Archiv für katholisches Kirchenrecht.*

ASS—*Acta Sanctae Sedis.*

Can. Canon.

Cans.—Canons.

Fontes—*Codicis Iuris Canonici Fontes cura . . . Gasparri editi.*

Mansi—*Sacrorum Conciliorum Nova et Amplissima Collectio.*

MPG—Migne, *Patrologia Graeca.*

MPL—Migne, *Patrologia Latina.*

NRT—*Nouvelle Revue Théologique.*

Pont. Comm. Intr.—Pontificia Commissio ad Codicis Canones authentica Interpretandas.

S.C.C.—Sacra Congregatio Concilii.

S.C.S.—Sacra Congregatio de disciplina Sacramentorum.

S.C.S.Off.—Suprema Congregatio Sancti Officii.

S.R.R.—Sacra Romana Rota.

S.R.R.Dec.—*Sacrae Romae Rotae Decisiones seu Sententiae.*

ALPHABETICAL INDEX

BIOGRAPHICAL NOTE

ADOLPH MARX was born February 18, 1915, in Cologne, Germany, where he received his primary education. In the fall of the year 1934 he entered St. Mary's University, La Porte, Texas, for his philosophical and theological studies. He was ordained to the Sacred Priesthood on May 2, 1940, by the Most Reverend E. B. Ledvina, D.D., LL.D., Bishop of Corpus Christi. In the fall of the same year he enrolled in the School of Canon Law at the Catholic University of America, and received the degree of the Baccalaureate in Canon Law in June, 1941, and the degree of the Licentiate in Canon Law in May, 1942.

CANON LAW STUDIES *

1. Frériks, Rev. Celestine A., C.PP.S., J.C.D., Religious Congregations in Their External Relations, 121 pp., 1916.
2. Galliher, Rev. Daniel M., O.P., J.C.D., Canonical Elections, 117 pp., 1917.
3. Borkowski, Rev. Aurelius L., O.F.M., J.C.D., De Confraternitatibus Ecclesiasticis, 136 pp., 1918.
4. Castillo, Rev. Cayo, J.C.D., Disertacion Historico-Canonica sobre la Potestad del Cabildo en Sede Vacante o Impedida del Vicario Capitular, 99 pp., 1919 (1918).
5. Kubelbeck, Rev. William J., S.T.B., J.C.D., The Sacred Penitentiaria and Its Relation to Faculties of Ordinaries and Priests, 129 pp., 1918.
6. Petrovits, Rev. Joseph, J.C., S.T.D., J.C.D., The New Church Law on Matrimony, X-461 pp., 1919.
7. Hickey, Rev. John J., S.T.B., J.C.D., Irregularities and Simple Impediments in the New Code of Canon Law, 100 pp., 1920.
8. Klekotka, Rev. Peter J., S.T.B., J.C.D., Diocesan Consultors, 179 pp., 1920.
9. Wanenmacher, Rev. Francis, J.C.D., The Evidence in Ecclesiastical Procedure Affecting the Marriage Bond, 1920 (Printed 1935).
10. Golden, Rev. Henry Francis, J.C.D., Parochial Benefices in the New Code, IV-119 pp., 1921 (Printed 1925).
11. Koudelka, Rev. Charles J., J.C.D., Pastors, Their Rights and Duties According to the New Code of Canon Law, 211 pp., 1921.
12. Melo, Rev. Antonius, O.F.M., J.C.D., De Exemptione Regularium, X-188 pp., 1921.
13. Schaaf, Rev. Valentine Theodore, O.F.M., S.T.B., J.C.D., The Cloister, X-180 pp., 1921.
14. Burke, Rev. Thomas Joseph, S.T.D., J.C.D., Competence in Ecclesiastical Tribunals, IV-117 pp., 1922.
15. Leech, Rev. George Leo, J.C.D., A Comparative Study of the Constitution "Apostolicae Sedis" and the "Codex Juris Canonici," 179 pp., 1922.
16. Motry, Rev. Hubert Louis, S.T.D., J.C.D., Diocesan Faculties According to the Code of Canon Law, II-167 pp., 1922.
17. Murphy, Rev. George Lawrence, J.C.D., Delinquencies and Penalties in the Administration and the Reception of the Sacraments, IV-121 pp., 1923.
18. O'Reilly, Rev. John Anthony, S.T.B., J.C.D., Ecclesiastical Sepulture in the New Code of Canon Law, II-129 pp., 1923.

* Below n. 100 only the following numbers are still available: Nn. 3, 4, 9, 25, 34, 57 and 75. Beginning with n. 100 only the following are unavailable: Nn. 100, 101, 102, 104, 105, 107, 108, 109, 111 and 113.

19. Michalicka, Rev. Wenceslas Cyrill, O.S.B., J.C.D., Judicial Procedure in Dismissal of Clerical Exempt Religious, 107 pp., 1923.
20. Dargin, Rev. Edward Vincent, S.T.B., J.C.D., Reserved Cases According to the Code of Canon Law, IV-103 pp., 1924.
21. Godfrey, Rev. John A., S.T.B., J.C.D., The Right of Patronage According to the Code of Canon Law, 153 pp., 1924.
22. Hagedorn, Rev. Francis Edward, J.C.D., General Legislation on Indulgences, II-154 pp., 1924.
23. King, Rev. James Ignatius, J.C.D., The Administration of the Sacraments to Dying Non-Catholics, V-141 pp., 1924.
24. Winslow, Rev. Francis Joseph, O.F.M., J.C.D., Vicars and Prefects Apostolic, IV-149 pp., 1924.
25. Correa, Rev. Jose Servelion, S.T.L., J.C.D., La Potestad Legislativa de la Iglesia Catolica, IV-127 pp., 1925.
26. Dugan, Rev. Henry Francis, A.M., J.C.D., The Judiciary Department of the Diocesan Curia, 87 pp., 1925.
27. Keller, Rev. Charles Frederick, S.T.B., J.C.D., Mass Stipends, 167 pp., 1925.
28. Paschang, Rev. John Linus, J.C.D., The Sacramentals According to the Code of Canon Law, 129 pp., 1925.
29. Piontek, Rev. Cyrillus, O.F.M., S.T.B., J.C.D., De Indulto Exclaustrationis necnon Saecularizationis, XIII-289 pp., 1925.
30. Kearney, Rev. Richard Joseph, S.T.B., J.C.D., Sponsors at Baptism According to the Code of Canon Law, IV-127 pp., 1925.
31. Bartlett, Rev. Chester Joseph, A.M., LL.B., J.C.D., The Tenure of Parochial Property in the United States of America, V-108 pp., 1926.
32. Kilker, Rev. Adrian Jerome, J.C.D., Extreme Unction, V-425 pp., 1926.
33. McCormick, Rev. Robert Emmett, J.C.D., Confessors of Religious, VIII-266 pp., 1926.
34. Miller, Rev. Newton Thomas, J.C.D., Founded Masses According to the Code of Canon Law, VII-93 pp., 1926.
35. Roelker, Rev. Edward G., S.T.D., J.C.D., Principles of Privilege According to the Code of Canon Law, XI-166 pp., 1926.
36. Bakalarczyk, Rev. Richardus, M.I.C., J.U.D., De Novitiatu, VIII-208 pp., 1927.
37. Pizzuti, Rev. Lawrence, O.F.M., J.U.L., De Parochis Religiosis, 1927. (Not Printed.)
38. Bliley, Rev. Nicholas Martin, O.S.B., J.C.D., Altars According to the Code of Canon Law, XIX-132 pp., 1927.
39. Brown, Mr. Brendan Francis, A.B., LL.M., J.U.D., The Canonical Juristic Personality with Special Reference to its Status in the United States of America, V-212 pp., 1927.
40. Cavanaugh, Rev. William Thomas, C.P., J.U.D., The Reservation of the Blessed Sacrament, VIII-101 pp., 1927.

41. DOHENY, REV. WILLIAM J., C.S.C., A.B., J.U.D., Church Property: Modes of Acquisition, X-118 pp., 1927.
42. FELDHAUS, REV. ALOYSIUS H., C.PP.S., J.C.D., Oratories, IX-141 pp., 1927.
43. KELLY, REV. JAMES PATRICK, A.B., J.C.D., The Jurisdiction of the Simple Confessor, X-208 pp., 1927.
44. NEUBERGER, REV. NICHOLAS J., J.C.D., Canon 6 or the Relation of the Codex Juris Canonici to the Preceding Legislation, V-95 pp., 1927.
45. O'KEEFE, REV. GERALD MICHAEL, J.C.D., Matrimonial Dispensations, Powers of Bishops, Priests, and Confessors, VIII-232 pp., 1927.
46. QUIGLEY, REV. JOSEPH A. M., A.B., J.C.D., Condemned Societies, 139 pp., 1927.
47. ZAPLOTNIK, REV. JOHANNES LEO, J.C.D., De Vicariis Foraneis, X-142 pp., 1927.
48. DUSKIE, REV. JOHN ALOYSIUS, A.B., J.C.D., The Canonical Status of the Orientals in the United States, VIII-196 pp., 1928.
49. HYLAND, REV. FRANCIS EDWARD, J.C.D., Excommunciation, Its Nature, Historical Development and Effects, VIII-181 pp., 1928.
50. REINMANN, REV. GERALD JOSEPH, O.M.C., J.C.D., The Third Order Secular of Saint Francis, 201 pp., 1928.
51. SCHENK, REV. FRANCIS J., J.C.D., The Matrimonial Impediments of Mixed Religion and Disparity of Cult, XVI-318 pp., 1929.
52. COADY, REV. JOHN JOSEPH, S.T.D., J.U.D., A.M., The Appointment of Pastors, VIII-150 pp., 1929.
53. KAY, REV. THOMAS HENRY, J.C.D., Competence in Matrimonial Procedure, VIII-164 pp., 1929.
54. TURNER, REV. SIDNEY JOSEPH, C.P., J.U.D., The Vow of Poverty, XLIX-217 pp., 1929.
55. KEARNEY, REV. RAYMOND A., A.B., S.T.D., J.C.D., The Principles of Delegation, VII-149 pp., 1929.
56. CONRAN, REV. EDWARD JAMES, A.B., J.C.D., The Interdict, V-163 pp., 1930.
57. O'NEILL, REV. WILLIAM H., J.C.D., Papal Rescripts of Favor, VII-218 pp., 1930.
58. BASTNAGEL, REV. CLEMENT VINCENT, J.U.D., The Appointment of Parochial Adjutants and Assistants, XV-257 pp., 1930.
59. FERRY, REV. WILLIAM A., A.B., J.C.D., Stole Fees, V-136 pp., 1930.
60. COSTELLO, REV. JOHN MICHAEL, A.B., J.C.D., Domicile and Quasi-Domicile, VII-201 pp., 1930.
61. KREMER, REV. MICHAEL NICHOLAS, A.B., S.T.B., J.C.D., Church Support in the United States, VI-136 pp., 1930.
62. ANGULO, REV. LUIS, C.M., J.C.D., Legislation de la Iglesia sobre la intencion en la application de la Santa Misa, VII-104 pp., 1931.
63. FREY, REV. WOLFGANG NORBERT, O.S.B., A.B., J.C.D., The Act of Religious Profession, VIII-174 pp., 1931.

64. Roberts, Rev. James Brendan, A.B., J.C.D., The Banns of Marriage, XIV-140 pp., 1931.

65. Ryder, Rev. Raymond Aloysius, A.B., J.C.D., Simony, IX-151 pp., 1931.

66. Campagna, Rev. Angelo, Ph.D., J.U.D., Il Vicario Generale del Vescovo, VII-205 pp., 1931.

67. Cox, Rev. Joseph Godfrey, A.B., J.C.D., The Administration of Seminaries, VI-124 pp., 1931.

68. Gregory, Rev. Donald J., J.U.D., The Pauline Privilege, XV-165 pp., 1931.

69. Donohue, Rev. John F., J.C.D., The Impediment of Crime, VII-110 pp., 1931.

70. Dooley, Rev. Eugene A., O.M.I., J.C.D., Church Law on Sacred Relics, IX-143 pp., 1931.

71. Orth, Rev. Clement Raymond, O.M.C., J.C.D., The Approbation of Religious Institutes, 171 pp., 1931.

72. Pernicone, Rev. Joseph M., A.B., J.C.D., The Ecclesiastical Prohibition of Books, XII-267 pp., 1932.

73. Clinton, Rev. Connell, A.B., J.C.D., The Paschal Precept, IX-108 pp., 1932.

74. Donnelly, Rev. Francis B., A.M., S.T.L., J.C.D., The Diocesan Synod, VIII-125 pp., 1932.

75. Torrente, Rev. Camilo, C.M.F., J.C.D., Las Processiones Sagradas, V-145 pp., 1932.

76. Murphy, Rev. Edwin J., C.PP.S., J.C.D., Suspension Ex Informata Conscientia, XI-122 pp., 1932.

77. MacKenzie, Rev. Eric F., A.M., S.T.L., J.C.D., The Delict of Heresy in its Commission, Penalization, Absolution, VII-124 pp., 1932.

78. Lyons, Rev. Avitus E., S.T.B., J.C.D., The Collegiate Tribunal of First Instance, XI-147 pp., 1932.

79. Connolly, Rev. Thomas A., J.C.D., Appeals, XI-195 pp., 1932.

80. Sangmeister, Rev. Joseph V., A.B., J.C.D., Force and Fear as Precluding Matrimonial Consent, V-211 pp., 1932.

81. Jaeger, Rev. Leo A., A.B., J.C.D., The Administration of Vacant and Quasi-Vacant Episcopal Sees in the United States, IX-229 pp., 1932.

82. Rimlinger, Rev. Herbert T., J.C.D., Error Invalidating Matrimonial Consent, VII-79 pp., 1932.

83. Barrett, Rev. John D. M., S.S., J.C.D., A Comparative Study of the Third Plenary Council of Baltimore and the Code, IX-221 pp., 1932.

84. Carberry, Rev. John J., Ph.D., S.T.D., J.C.D., The Juridical Form of Marriage, X-177 pp., 1934.

85. Dolan, Rev. John L., A.B., J.C.D., The Defensor Vinculi, XII-157 pp., 1934.

86. Hannan, Rev. Jerome D., A.M., S.T.D., LL.B., J.C.D., The Canon Law of Wills, IX-517 pp., 1934.

87. LEMIEUX, REV. DELISE A., A.M., J.C.D., The Sentence in Ecclesiastical Procedure, IX-131 pp., 1934.
88. O'ROURKE, REV. JAMES J., A.B., J.C.D., Parish Registers, VII-109 pp., 1934.
89. TIMLIN, REV. BARTHOLOMEW, O.F.M., A.M., J.C.D., Conditional Matrimonial Consent, X-381 pp., 1934.
90. WAHL, REV. FRANCIS X., A.B., J.C.D., The Matrimonial Impediments of Consanguinity and Affinity, VI-125 pp., 1934.
91. WHITE, REV. ROBERT J., A.B., LL.B., S.T.B., J.C.D., Canonical Ante-Nuptial Promises and the Civil Law, VI-152 pp., 1934.
92. HERRERA, REV. ANTONIO PARRA, O.C.D., J.C.D., Legislacion Ecclesiastica sobra el Ayuno y la Abstinencia, XI-191 pp., 1935.
93. KENNEDY, REV. EDWIN J., J.C.D., The Special Matrimonial Process in Cases of Evident Nullity, X-165 pp., 1935.
94. MANNING, REV. JOHN J., A.B., J.C.D., Presumption of Law in Matrimonial Procedure, XI-111 pp., 1935.
95. MOEDER, REV. JOHN M., J.C.D., The Proper Bishop for Ordination and Dimissorial Letters, VII-135 pp., 1935.
96. O'MARA, REV. WILLIAM A., A.B., J.C.D., Canonical Causes for Matrimonial Dispensations, IX-155 pp., 1935.
97. REILLY, REV. PETER, J.C.D., Residence of Pastors, IX-81 pp., 1935.
98. SMITH, REV. MARINER T., O.P., S.T.Lr., J.C.D., The Penal Law for Religious, VII-169 pp., 1935.
99. WHALEN, REV. DONALD W., A.M., J.C.D., The Value of Testimonial Evidence in Matrimonial Procedure, XIII-297 pp., 1935.
100. CLEARY, REV. JOSEPH F., J.C.D., Canonical Limitations on the Alienation of Church Property, VIII-141 pp., 1936.
101. GLYNN, REV. JOHN C., J.C.D., The Promoter of Justice, XX-337 pp., 1936.
102. BRENNAN, REV. JAMES H., S.S., M.A., S.T.B., J.C.D., The Simple Convalidation of Marriage, VI-135 pp., 1937.
103. BRUNINI, REV. JOSEPH BERNARD, J.C.D., The Clerical Obligations of Canons 139 and 142, X-121 pp., 1937.
104. CONNOR, REV. MAURICE, A.B., J.C.D., The Administrative Removal of Pastors, VIII-159 pp., 1937.
105. GUILFOYLE, REV. MERLIN JOSEPH, J.C.D., Custom, XI-144 pp., 1937.
106. HUGHES, REV. JAMES AUSTIN, A.B., A.M., J.C.D., Witnesses in Criminal Trials of Clerics, IX-140 pp., 1937.
107. JANSEN, REV. RAYMOND J., A.B., S.T.L., J.C.D., Canonical Provisions for Catechetical Instruction, VII-153 pp., 1937.
108. KEALY, REV. JOHN JAMES, A.B., J.C.D., The Introductory Libellus in Church Court Procedure, XI-121 pp., 1937.
109. McMANUS, REV. JAMES EDWARD, C.SS.R., J.C.D., The Administration of Temporal Goods in Religious Institutes, XVI-196 pp., 1937.

110. Moriarty, Rev. Eugene James, J.C.D., Oaths in Ecclesiastical Courts, X-115 pp., 1937.

111. Rainer, Rev. Eligius George, C.SS.R., J.C.D., Suspension of Clerics, XVII-249 pp., 1937.

112. Reilly, Rev. Thomas F., C.SS.R., J.C.D., Visitation of Religious, VI-195 pp., 1938.

113. Moriarty, Rev. Francis E., C.SS.R., J.C.D., The Extraordinary Absolution from Censures, XV-334 pp., 1938.

114. Connolly, Rev. Nicholas P., J.C.D., The Canonical Erection of Parishes, X-132 pp., 1938.

115. Donovan, Rev. James Joseph, J.C.D., The Pastor's Obligation in Prenuptial Investigation, XII-322 pp., 1938.

116. Harrigan, Rev. Robert J., M.A., S.T.B., J.C.D., The Radical Sanation of Invalid Marriages, VIII-208 pp., 1938.

117. Boffa, Rev. Conrad Humbert, J.C.D., Canonical Provisions for Catholic Schools, VII-211 pp., 1939.

118. Parsons, Rev. Anscar John, O.M.Cap., J.C.D., Canonical Elections, XII-236 pp., 1939.

119. Reilly, Rev. Edward Michael, A.B., J.C.D., The General Norms of Dispensation, XII-156 pp., 1939.

120. Ryan, Rev. Gerald Aloysius, A.B., J.C.D., Principles of Episcopal Jurisdiction, XII-172 pp., 1939.

121. Burton, Rev. Francis James, C.S.C., A.B., J.C.D., A Commentary on Canon 1125, X-222 pp., 1940.

122. Miaskiewicz, Rev. Francis Sigismund, J.C.D., Supplied Jurisdiction According to Canon 209, XII-340 pp., 1940.

123. Rice, Rev. Patrick William, A.B., J.C.D., Proof of Death in Prenuptial Investigation, VIII-156 pp., 1940.

124. Anglin, Rev. Thomas Francis, M.S., J.C.D., The Eucharistic Fast, VIII-183 pp., 1941.

125. Coleman, Rev. John Jerome, J.C.D., The Minister of Confirmation, VI-153 pp., 1941.

126. Downs, Rev. Joseph Emmanuel, A.B., J.C.D., The Concept of Clerical Immunity, XI-163 pp., 1941.

127. Esswein, Rev. Anthony Albert, J.C.D., Extrajudicial Penal Powers of Ecclesiastical Superiors, X-144 pp., 1941.

128. Farrell, Rev. Benjamin Francis, M.A., S.T.L., J.C.D., The Rights and Duties of the Local Ordinary Regarding Congregations of Women Religious of Pontifical Approval, V-195 pp., 1941.

129. Feeney, Rev. Thomas John, A.B., S.T.L., J.C.D., Restitutio in Integrum, VI-169 pp., 1941.

130. Findlay, Rev. Stephen William, O.S.B., A.B., J.C.D., Canonical Norms Governing the Deposition and Degradation of Clerics, XVII-279 pp., 1941.

131. GOODWINE, REV. JOHN, A.B., S.T.L., J.C.D., The Right of the Church to Acquire Property, VIII-119 pp., 1941.
132. HESTON, REV. EDWARD LOUIS, C.S.C., Ph.D., S.T.D., J.C.D., The Alienation of Church Property in the United States, XII-222 pp., 1941.
133. HOGAN, REV. JAMES JOHN, A.B., S.T.L., J.C.D., Judicial Advocates and Procurators, XIII-200 pp., 1941.
134. KEALY, REV. THOMAS M., A.B., Litt.B., J.C.D., Dowry of Women Religious, IX-152 pp., 1941.
135. KEENE, REV. MICHAEL JAMES, O.S.B., J.C.D., Religious Ordinaries and Canon 198, V-164 pp., 1942.
136. KERIN, REV. CHARLES A., S.S., M.A., S.T.B., J.C.D., The Privation of Christian Burial, XVI-279 pp., 1941.
137. LOUIS, REV. WILLIAM FRANCIS, M.A., J.C.D., Diocesan Archives, X-101 pp., 1941.
138. McDEVITT, REV. GILBERT JOSEPH, A.B., J.C.D., Legitimacy and Legitimation, X-247 pp., 1941.
139. McDONOUGH, REV. THOMAS JOSEPH, A.B., J.C.D., Apostolic Administrators, X-217 pp., 1941.
140. MEIER, REV. CARL ANTHONY, A.B., J.C.D., Penal Administration Procedure Against Negligent Pastors, XI-240 pp., 1941.
141. SCHMIDT, REV. JOHN ROGG, A.B., J.C.D., The Principles of Authentic Interpretation in Canon 17 of the Code of Canon Law, XII-331 pp., 1941.
142. SLAFKOSKY, REV. ANDREW LEONARD, A.B., J.C.D., The Canonical Episcopal Visitation of the Diocese, X-197 pp., 1941.
143. SWOBODA, REV. INNOCENT ROBERT, O.F.M., J.C.D., Ignorance in Relation to the Imputability of Delicts, IX-271 pp., 1941.
144. DUBÉ, REV. ARTHUR JOSEPH, A.B., J.C.D., The General Principles for the Reckoning of Time in Canon Law, VIII-299 pp., 1941.
145. McBRIDE, REV. JAMES T., A.B., J.C.D., Incardination and Excardination of Seculars, XX-585 pp., 1941.
146. KRÓL, REV. JOHN T., J.C.D., The Defendant in Ecclesiastical Trials, XII-207 pp., 1942.
147. COMYNS, REV. JOSEPH J., C.SS.R., A.B., J.C.D., Papal and Episcopal Administration of Church Property, XIV-155 pp., 1942.
148. BARRY, REV. GARRETT FRANCIS, O.M.I., J.C.D., Violation of the Cloister, XII-260 pp,, 1942.
149. BOLDUC, REV. GATIEN, C.S.V., A.B., S.T.L., J.C.D., Les Études dans les Religions Cléricales, VIII-155 pp., 1942.
150. BOYLE, REV. DAVID JOHN, M.A., J.C.D., The Juridic Effects of Moral Certitude on Pre-Nuptial Guarantees, XII-188 pp., 1942.
151. CANAVAN, REV. WALTER JOSEPH, M.A., LITT.D., J.C.D., The Profession of Faith, XII-143 pp., 1942.
152. DESROCHERS, REV. BRUNO, A.B., PH.L., S.T.B., J.C.D., Le Premier Concile Plénier de Québec et le Code de Droit Canonique, XIV-186 pp., 1942.

153. Dillon, Rev. Robert Edward, A.B., J.C.D., Common Law Marriage, X-148 pp., 1942.
154. Dodwell, Rev. Edward John, Ph.D., S.T.B., J.C.L., The Time and Place for the Celebration of Marriage.
155. Donnellan, Rev. Thomas Andrew, A.B., J.C.D., The Obligation of the Missa pro Populo, VII-131 pp., 1942.
156. Eltz, Rev. Louis Anthony, A.B., J.C.L., Cooperation in Crime.
157. Gass, Rev. Sylvester Francis, M.A., J.C.D., Ecclesiastical Pensions, XI-206 pp., 1942.
158. Guiniven, Rev. John Joseph, C.SS.R., J.C.D., The Precept of Hearing Mass, XIV-188 pp., 1942.
159. Gulczynski, Rev. John Theophilus, J.C.L., The Desecration and Violation of Churches.
160. Hammill, Rev. John Leo, M.A., J.C.D., The Obligations of the Traveler According to Canon 14, VIII-204 pp., 1942.
161. Haydt, Rev. John Joseph, A.B., J.C.D., Reserved Benefices, XI-148 pp., 1942.
162. Huser, Rev. Roger John, O.F.M., A.B., J.C.L., The Crime of Abortion in Canon Law.
163. Kearney, Rev. Francis Patrick, A.B., S.T.L., J.C.L., The Principles of Canon 1127.
164. Linahen, Rev. Leo James, S.T.L., J.C.D., De Absolutione Complicis In Peccato Turpi, 114 pp., 1942.
165. McCloskey, Rev. Joseph Aloysius, A.B., J.C.D., The Subject of Ecclesiastical Law According to Canon 12, XVII-246 pp., 1942.
166. O'Neill, Rev. Francis Joseph, C.SS.R., J.C.D., The Dismissal of Religious in Temporary Vows, XIII-220 pp., 1942.
167. Prince, Rev. John Edward, A.B., S.T.B., J.C.D., The Diocesan Chancellor, X-136 pp., 1942.
168. Riesner, Rev. Albert Joseph, C.SS.R., J.C.D., Apostates and Fugitives from Religious Institutes, IX-168 pp., 1942.
169. Stenger, Rev. Joseph Bernard, J.C.D., The Mortgaging of Church Property, 186 pp., 1942.
170. Waldron, Rev. Joseph Francis, A.B., J.C.D., The Minister of Baptism, XII-197 pp., 1942.
171. Willett, Rev. Robert Albert, J.C.D., The Probative Value of Documents in Ecclesiastical Trials, X-124 pp., 1942.
172. Woeber, Rev. Edward Martin, M.A., J.C.D., The Interpellations, XII-161 pp., 1942.
173. Benko, Rev. Matthew Aloysius, O.S.B., M.A., J.C.L., The Abbot *Nullius*.
174. Christ, Rev. Joseph James, M.A., S.T.L., J.C.L., Dispensation from Vindicative Penalties.
175. Clancy, Rev. Patrick M. J., O.P., A.B., S.T.Lr., J.C.L., The Local Religious Superior.

176. Clarke, Rev. Thomas James, J.C.L., Parish Societies.
177. Connolly, Rev. John Patrick, S.T.L., J.C.L., Synodal Examiners and Parish Priest Consultors.
178. Drumm, Rev. William Martin, A.B., J.C.L., Hospital Chaplains.
179. Flanagan, Rev. Bernard Joseph, A.B., S.T.L., J.C.L., The Canonical Erection of Religious Houses.
180. Kelleher, Rev. Stephen Joseph, A.B., S.T.B., J.C.L., Discussions with non-Catholics: Canonical Legislation.
181. Lewis, Rev. Gordian, C.P., J.C.L., Chapters in Religious Institutes.
182. Marx, Rev. Adolph, J.C.L., The Declaration of Nullity of Marriages Contracted Outside the Church.
183. Matulenas, Rev. Raymond Anthony, O.S.B., A.B., J.C.L., Communication, a Source of Privileges.
184. O'Leary, Rev. Charles Gerard, C.SS.R., Religious Dismissed After Perpetual Profession.
185. Power, Rev. Cornelius Michael, J.C.L., The Blessing of Cemeteries.
186. Shuhler, Rev. Ralph Vincent, O.S.A., J.C.L., Privileges of Religious to Absolve and Dispense.
187. Ziolkowski, Rev. Thaddeus Stanislaus, A.B., J.C.L., The Consecration and Blessing of Churches.

www.ingramcontent.com/pod-product-compliance
Lightning Source LLC
LaVergne TN
LVHW050222080826
844660LV00012B/456

* 9 7 8 0 8 1 3 2 2 3 7 1 1 *